Religion in America

SOCIOLOGY IN THE TWENTY-FIRST CENTURY

Edited by John Iceland, Pennsylvania State University

This series introduces students to a range of sociological issues of broad interest in the United States today and addresses topics such as race, immigration, gender, the family, education, and social inequality. Each work has a similar structure and approach as follows:

- introduction to the topic's importance in contemporary society
- overview of conceptual issues
- review of empirical research including demographic data
- cross-national comparisons
- discussion of policy debates

These course books highlight findings from current, rigorous research and include personal narratives to illustrate major themes in an accessible manner. The similarity in approach across the series allows instructors to assign them as a featured or supplementary book in various courses.

1. *A Portrait of America: The Demographic Perspective,* by John Iceland
2. *Race and Ethnicity in America,* by John Iceland
3. *Education in America,* by Kimberly A. Goyette
4. *Families in America,* by Susan L. Brown
5. *Population Health in America,* by Robert A. Hummer and Erin R. Hamilton
6. *Religion in America,* by Lisa D. Pearce and Claire Chipman Gilliland

Religion in America

Lisa D. Pearce and
Claire C. Gilliland

UNIVERSITY OF CALIFORNIA PRESS

University of California Press
Oakland, California

© 2020 by the Regents of the University of California

Sociology in the Twenty-First Century, 6

Library of Congress Cataloging-in-Publication Data

Names: Pearce, Lisa D. (Lisa Deanne), 1971– author. | Gilliland, Claire C.,
    author.
Title: Religion in America / Lisa D. Pearce and Claire C. Gilliland.
Other titles: Sociology in the 21st century (University of California
    Press) ; 6.
Description: Oakland, California : University of California Press,
    [2020] | Series: Sociology in the twenty-first century; 6 |
    Includes bibliographical references and index.
Identifiers: LCCN 2019059455 (print) | LCCN 2019059456 (ebook) |
    ISBN 9780520296411 (cloth) | ISBN 9780520296428 (paperback) |
    ISBN 9780520968929 (ebook)
Subjects: LCSH: Religion and sociology—United States. | Religion and
    politics—United States. | United States—Religious life and customs—
    History.
Classification: LCC BL2525 .P43 2020 (print) | LCC BL2525 (ebook) |
    DDC 200.973/09051—dc23
LC record available at https://lccn.loc.gov/2019059455
LC ebook record available at https://lccn.loc.gov/2019059456

Manufactured in the United States of America

28 27 26 25 24 23 22 21 20
10 9 8 7 6 5 4 3 2 1

Contents

List of Figures, Tables, and Text Boxes   vii

Acknowledgments   xi

Introduction   1

1. Racial and Ethnic Variation in Religion and Its Trends   19

2. Complex Religion in America   37

3. A Demographic Perspective on Religious Change   56

4. Change in America's Congregations   83

5. The Long Arm of Religion in America   102

    Conclusion   125

Notes   137

References   155

Index   183

Figures, Tables, and Text Boxes

FIGURES

1. Aggregate Religiosity Index (ARI), United States, 1952–2005   10

2. Rate of religious service attendance by race, United States, 1972–2018   28

3. Rate of prayer by race, United States, 1983–2018   29

4. Trends in Latinx religious affiliation, United States, 2000–2018   30

5. Weekly rate of religious service attendance by education level, United States, 1972–2018   40

6. Daily rate of prayer by education level, United States, 1983–2018   41

7. Proportion of population with no religious affiliation by gender, United States, 1972–2018   46

8. Weekly rate of religious service attendance by gender, United States, 1972–2018   46

9. Proportion with no religious affiliation by combined race, education, and gender groups, United States, 1972–2018   50

10. Average rates of religious service attendance by combined race, education, and gender groups, United States, 1972–2018   52

11. Average rates of prayer by combined race, education, and gender groups, United States, 1983–2018   53

12. Percentage of women affiliated with religious traditions in 1977, 2018, and predicted levels in 2018 if demographic characteristic shown remained at 1977 levels, United States   72

13. Percentage of men affiliated with religious traditions in 1977, 2018, and predicted levels in 2018 if demographic characteristic shown remained at 1977 levels, United States   72

14. Increasing ethnic diversity in predominantly White congregations, United States   92

15. Sample headlines following the 2016 election of Donald Trump   103

16. Proportion of population with no religious preference by year and political views, United States, 1974–2012   104

17. Origins of the US immigrant population, 1960–2015   112

18. Correlations between religious service attendance and social conservatism, United States   119

TABLES

1. Trends in religious affiliation, United States, 1972–2016   8

2. Percentage not affiliated with any religion by age group and survey year, United States, 1976–2016   64

3. Predicted change over time in probability of religious service attendance in a given week if certain demographic changes had not occurred, United States, 1977–2018   77

4. Predicted change over time in probability of praying in a given day if certain demographic changes had not occurred, United States, 1977–2018   79

BOXES

1.   Social definitions of religion   4

2.   Race and religion in the United States: A historical perspective   35

3.   Gender, religiosity, and youth/young adults   45

4.   Cohort vs. generation   61

5.   Religious composition of countries around the world   82

6.   Geographic variation   85

7.   Exploring congregational data   99

8.   Personal religion and politics   105

9.   Religion in public blog   120

Acknowledgments

We are exceedingly grateful to the many people who played a part in the evolution of this book. First and foremost, for the invitation to participate in the community of scholars writing books for the Sociology in the Twenty-First Century series at the University of California Press, we thank John Iceland (series editor) and Naomi Schneider (executive editor). Their ideas, feedback, and support along the way have been invaluable. We also greatly appreciate the guidance and dedication of Benjy Mailings and Summer Farah (editorial assistants) in helping finalize all parts of the book, literally from the front to back cover. This book has greatly benefited from wise recommendations offered by Roger Finke, Jerry Park, Jenny Trinitapoli, and one anonymous reviewer along the way. Their much-appreciated insights helped enrich the development of the book and hone its core contributions.

We owe a great debt to our students, friends, and colleagues at the University of North Carolina at Chapel Hill. The curiosity and thoughtfulness of many of Lisa's *SOCI 429: Religion and Society* students served as inspiration and barometer for the book's content. Past and present graduate students, including Alyssa Browne, Erin Davenport, Reed DeAngelis, Katie Furl, George Hayward, Laura Krull, and Jane Lee all provided very helpful comments and edits in addition to moral support and encouragement all along the way. We owe Jessica Pearlman a great deal of thanks for her methodological expertise and her willingness to work with us on analyses for this book. Lisa is very grateful to Michele Berger and Karolyn Tyson for their insights and support in the writing process. Claire thanks her graduate student peers for their advice, perspectives, and listening ears at all stages of this project. We also thank Tania Jenkins for feedback on the conclusion. In general, we are fortunate to work in the incredibly generative and generous environments of the Department of Sociology and the Carolina Population Center where faculty, staff, and students make this work possible and rewarding.

At key moments in this journey, others stepped in to provide support. Jacquie and Nadine and the space and sustenance they provide at Easton's Nook sparked ideas and propelled the book's completion. We are also grateful to Kristy Johnson for her high-quality editing assistance with multiple chapters.

For all of these instrumental forms of support from friends and colleagues, we are forever thankful. The book has benefited greatly from their assistance. Any errors or oversights in the pages to come are owned fully by us.

Finally, we sincerely thank and express the full depth of our love and appreciation to our families for making our work and our lives richer. From the bottom of her heart, Lisa thanks Eric and Natalie for their love, grounding humor, and patience. Claire is grateful for Mac and for her family for their consistent support and love, and thanks her community of friends in Chapel Hill and beyond for their kindness and laughter.

Introduction

UNDERSTANDING RELIGION IN AMERICA

"In God We Trust" was first printed on US coins in 1864 during one of the most divisive periods of US history—the Civil War era. This motto endures as a symbol of both religion's importance in American society and religion's potential to unite and divide. Proponents of first placing "In God We Trust" on money considered it a national disgrace to not recognize God on US coins.[1] In a proposal to Congress, the secretary of the Treasury and the director of the US Mint characterized the addition to coins as "expressive of a national reliance on Divine protection, and a distinct and unequivocal national recognition of the Divine sovereignty—the claim to be a Christian nation."[2]

Abraham Lincoln was the first president of the United States to sign this act of Congress into law. Analyzing Lincoln's personal letters and Second Inaugural Address, Justin Latterell suggests that although most proponents for adding "In God We Trust" to coins appear to have done so out of nationalistic pride and as an appeal to God's favor toward the nation, Lincoln saw it as an assertion of humility.[3] Latterell argues that Lincoln likely understood the phrase as "a recognition of the inherent distinction between the providential will of God and the political wills of warring peoples."[4] These different interpretations of the same venerated phrase demonstrate the centrality of religion as a system of meaning in American life while at the same time revealing that religion is often understood and experienced by different Americans in different ways.

These four short words, "In God We Trust," have fallen in and out of favor over time and across regions, reflecting interesting dynamics and complexities in the religiousness of the US population. In 1909, President Theodore Roosevelt took the motto off two coins during a congressional recess, arguing that the motto on money was a form of irreverence that cheapened the phrase.[5] During the 1950s, a time of increased religious and nationalistic fervor in response to the Cold War and the spread of communism, "In God We Trust" was legislated as the official motto of the United States, and it was mandated that the motto appear on paper currency. Around the same time, the Pledge of Allegiance was revised to add the words "under God."[6] More recently, states such as Arkansas (in 2017) and Florida (in 2018) have mandated that "In God We Trust" be visibly displayed in their public schools. You can find the motto carved in stone on many public monuments, courthouses, and government buildings.

The history and use of these four words, "In God We Trust," reflect the long, dynamic, complex, and contested importance of religion, in particular Christianity, in American society. In the spirit of this observation, this book examines the changes over time, and the remarkable stability, in the religious composition and religiousness of America. We apply demographic, congregational, and historical perspectives to reveal rich and complex processes underlying previously documented, general trends for the entire US population. What results is a fuller picture of the people for whom religion is or is not changing, the engines for religious change where it occurs, how individual-level religious change shapes and is shaped by religious institutions, and religion's role in the distribution of power and influence in the United States.

DEFINING RELIGION AND RELIGIOUSNESS

In thinking about the state of religion in the United States, how do we define *religion*? Because religion is such an abstract concept, it is challenging to find a definition that is both broad enough to cover the variety of and diversity in world religions and specific enough to not include social institutions, belief systems, or rituals that are not generally understood as religions, such as magic or sports.

For centuries, scholars have been working out definitions of religion that guide social scientists. These definitions often reference *social groups or institutions* that unite around a certain set of *beliefs or practices* (see box 1 for a commonly referenced set of sociological definitions of religion). Thus, as we discuss religion throughout the book, we primarily focus on the social and institutional forms religions take and the beliefs and practices individuals hold.

Next, what exactly is *religiousness*, or the degree to which a person engages in religion? Think of the most religious person and the least religious person you know. What are the characteristics that make them more, or less, religious in your mind? Are you thinking of whether they consider themselves to belong to a certain religion or religious group? Are you considering how often they practice religion in a public way, maybe by attending worship services at a religious institution? Or, are you focused on more private practices such as prayer or meditation? Do you factor in how important religion seems to be in their lives? Maybe they are public about how religion shapes other aspects of their lives, including religious dress, eating or drinking restrictions, their sexual behavior, civic involvement, or their political views. It is probably some combination of these features of religiousness that everyone draws upon in classifying people religiously. Social scientists typically call these features *dimensions* of religiousness, and they are often interested in levels of these different dimensions in the population, such as average levels of religious service attendance, and the causes and consequences of any change in such levels.

At this point, you might be wondering how the concept of spirituality relates to religion or religiousness. Spirituality is a term that has grown in use since the 1970s, according to Google Books Ngram Viewer.[7] People define spirituality in a variety of ways. Some focus on practices or rituals conducted apart from major world religions in the interest of acknowledging or connecting with a divine force. These people often call themselves spiritual and not religious. Others use the concept of spirituality to characterize their own practice of a major world religion. In fact, many conservative Christians identify as spiritual and not religious to indicate a form of

Box 1 SOCIAL DEFINITIONS OF RELIGION

"Religion is the sigh of the oppressed creature, the sentiment of a heartless world, and the soul of soulless conditions. It is the opium of the people."—Karl Marx (1978 [1844], 54)

"A religion is a unified system of beliefs and practices relative to sacred things, that is to say, things set apart and forbidden—beliefs and practices which unite into a single moral community called a Church, all those who adhere to them."—Emile Durkheim (1995 [1912], 44)

Religion is "a set of symbolic forms and acts that relate [people] to the ultimate conditions of [their] existence."—Robert Bellah (1964, 359)

"Religion is the human enterprise by which a sacred cosmos is established. . . . By sacred is meant here a quality of mysterious and awesome power, other than man and yet related to him, which is believed to reside in certain objects of experience."—Peter Berger (1967, 25)

"Religion, then, can be defined as a system of beliefs and practices by means of which a group of people struggles with these ultimate problems of human life. It expresses their refusal to capitulate to death, to give up in the face of frustration, to allow hostility to tear apart their human associations."—J. Milton Yinger (1970, 7)

"Religion is (1) a system of symbols which acts to (2) establish powerful, pervasive, and long lasting moods and motivations in [people] by (3) formulating conceptions of a general order of existence and (4) clothing these conceptions with such an aura of factuality that the moods and motivations seem uniquely realistic."—Clifford Geertz (1973, 90)

"Religion is a complex of culturally prescribed practices, based on premises about the existence and nature of superhuman powers, whether personal or impersonal, which seek to help practitioners gain access to and communicate or align themselves with these powers, in hopes of realizing human goods and avoiding things bad."—Christian Smith (2017, 22) faith or devotion that is personal, based on a connection with God, and not ritualistic. Most people in the United States, however, identify as spiritual *and* religious. Spirituality is associated with personal experiences of transcendence or meaningfulness through divine connection.[8] Religion or religiousness is associated with structured, institutionally supported beliefs and behaviors that connect one human being to others and provide a roadmap for how to live.[9] Although we do occasionally discuss spirituality, for most of the book we focus on the concepts of religion and religiousness, which include forms of spirituality that overlap with or are understood as occurring in connection to religion.

MEASURING CHANGE IN AMERICAN RELIGION

The most common approach to tracking the religious character of America, at least in recent times, has been the use of national survey data to analyze self-reports of religious affiliation, frequency of religious service attendance, rates of prayer, and strength of beliefs. Most studies of this type describe trends from the 1970s forward because the longest-running, highest-quality data available on religious trends come from the General Social Survey (GSS), which started in 1972.[10] The GSS is a nationally representative survey that has been systematically fielded at least every other year since 1972. Questions on the GSS measure social attitudes, religious beliefs and behaviors, and demographic characteristics like racial/ethnic identity or educational attainment. With national surveys like the GSS or the National Congregations Study (NCS), social scientists can study how religious attitudes and behaviors are related to other important social factors, such as political affiliation, and track changes over time in individual-level beliefs or organizational characteristics.

Throughout this book, we also refer to research using forms of data other than surveys, like ethnographic research involving fieldnotes and interviews; less structured, interview-based studies that result in qualitative data for analysis; or comparative-historical research using archival data. Although research relying on methods such as these is often not statistically generalizable, it does contribute in ways that survey research often cannot, in part by offering the ability to discover and richly describe meanings and processes that are at the core of religious belief and practice and that are not well anticipated or measured in survey research.

Although the reliance on survey data from the past forty or so years is partly driven by using the most comprehensive and nationally representative survey data available, there are other reasons this time span is an appropriate historical focus. Poll data suggest that religiousness rose to a relative high in the 1960s, and a great deal of social change of the type that is assumed to alter the authority and practice of religion in society has occurred since then. These changes (which are highly interrelated themselves) include the increasing racial and ethnic diversity of the United States, dramatic increases in educational attainment and women's labor force participation, the sexual revolution and the availability of contraception, and family changes such as the postponement of marriage and childbearing, reduced fertility, and increases in divorce, nonmarital cohabitation, and nonmarital childbearing.

The dimensions of religion or religiousness most consistently measured in the GSS are, not surprisingly, the most commonly analyzed in the field, so they are the main focus of both the studies we review and the original analyses we share in this book. These include self-identified religious affiliation, self-reported frequency of religious service attendance, and self-reported frequency of prayer.

GENERAL TRENDS IN RELIGION IN AMERICA

In the substantive chapters of this book, we will demonstrate that population-level analyses of religious trends over time—for example, looking at the average number of times all Americans attend religious services in a month—gloss over much of the richness and complexity that make religion in the United States interesting. This is because there are distinctive patterns for different groups in the United States, including variations across racial and ethnic groups, particularities in the religious involvement of young and old people, and changes in the nature of congregations in which people worship. Similarly, these analyses ignore the role religion plays in American history and in what ways religion continues to draw dividing lines between groups of people. However, in order to document this variation in subsequent chapters, it is helpful to first establish some basic trends in the United States as a whole to help understand why the variation we uncover later is relevant to the story of religion in America.

Two of the most substantial changes in the American religious landscape of late pertain to how Americans affiliate themselves religiously.[11] First, the percentage of the population identifying with a mainstream, or what most researchers term a mainline Protestant group (e.g., members of the United Methodist Church, the Evangelical Lutheran Church of America, or the Presbyterian Church (USA), among others),[12] has shrunk in half from just over 25 percent in 1972 to 13 percent in 2014.[13] Second, the percentage of Americans who have no religious affiliation has tripled, growing from around 6 percent in 1972 to 20 percent in 2014.[14] Scholars sometimes refer to people who report no religious affiliation as the religious "Nones" (Not to be confused with religious N-U-N-S!), but we will refer to them as the "religiously unaffiliated." We use that term to be as precise as possible because having no institutional affiliation does not necessarily mean a person has no religious beliefs or practices.[15] There has been relative stability in the percentage of Americans who identify with conservative or Evangelical Protestant groups, like Southern Baptists, Pentecostals, and many non-denominational churches. The same has been true for Catholics. Each group has made up almost a quarter of the US population over time.[16]

Because the United States has been heralded as a religiously diverse nation since its beginning, many people are surprised to discover just how small the proportions of Jewish, Latter-day Saint (Mormon), Hindu, Muslim, and Buddhist affiliates remain in the US population (see table 1). The Jewish population has seen a slight decline over the past few decades, a decline largely attributed to growing numbers of young people who identify as Jewish ethnically, but not religiously.[17] On the other hand, although they are still a very small part of the US population, Hindus, Muslims, and Buddhists have grown in number since the 2000s. This almost entirely stems from these religious groups' increased immigration to the United States from countries where their religions are predominant.

When it comes to rates of religious practice in the United States, recent studies suggest there has been a slight overall decline in the population

Table 1   Trends in religious affiliation, United States, 1972–2016 (General Social Survey); N=59,205

Religious Affiliation	1970s (%)	1980s (%)	1990s (%)	2000s (%)	2010s (%)
Evangelical Protestant	21.96	26.61	27.57	25.70	25.20
Mainline Protestant	29.23	23.47	19.32	15.32	12.44
Black Protestant	9.31	8.02	8.31	8.07	7.02
Catholic	27.08	27.19	26.11	27.06	25.91
Jewish	2.35	2.04	1.99	2.00	1.77
Latter-day Saints	0.79	2.17	1.26	1.30	1.04
Hindu	NA	NA	0.06	0.37	0.48
Muslim	NA	NA	0.12	0.61	0.71
Buddhist	NA	NA	0.06	0.72	0.80
Other religion	2.42	3.11	4.74	3.12	3.25
No religious affiliation	6.85	7.40	10.46	15.73	21.38

NOTE: The first five categories of affiliation are coded as recommended by Steensland et al. (2000) and Stetzer and Burge (2016). The remaining categories are coded as reported, except the "Other" category, which is a combination of remaining smaller religious groups. Hindu, Buddhist, and Muslim were not added as religious traditions in the GSS until 1998.

average of religious service attendance over the past four decades.[18] The average level of prayer has seen a statistically significant decrease since 1988; however, the year-by-year trends show many offsetting increases and decreases.[19] Wachholtz and Sambamoorthi, for example, found an increase in the percentage of people in the United States who reported praying about their mental or physical health between 2001 and 2007.[20] The steepest decline in the average frequency of prayer has really taken place over the past ten years or so; it thus remains to be seen whether that trend will continue into the next decade.

Findings from the World Values Survey show that among postindustrial countries, the United States has some of the highest levels of religious participation and frequency of prayer, levels similar to those found in Ireland and Italy, two steadfastly Catholic countries. By comparison, France, Denmark, and Great Britain show the lowest levels—at least of these indicators of religiousness.[21]

An additional barometer by which to assess religious change in the United States over time is to look at how individuals have responded to questions about their beliefs in certain religious concepts or ideas. The proportion of adults in the United States who believe in life after death has been increasing since the 1970s, from 75 percent at that time to 80 percent in 2014.[22] There is little evidence of a population-level decline in *some* belief in God across time.[23] However, there has been a downturn in *absolute* belief in God, from around 65 percent (where it had generally held since 1988) in 2000 to 58 percent in 2014.[24] Also, the percentage of those who believe the Bible is to be taken literally has declined from just under 40 percent in the 1980s to just under 35 percent in the 1990s, dropping closer to 30 percent in the 2000s.[25] In short, the evidence we have from the GSS and other data suggests that some religious beliefs are as strong today as they were over four decades ago while other beliefs have weakened.[26]

Compared to other wealthy Western countries, the United States holds very high average levels of religious belief.[27] Two other countries in which approximately 95 percent of the population believed in God in 1947, Canada and Australia, experienced declines to 88 and 75 percent, respectively, while the United States maintained that level through 2001.[28] When it comes to the percentage of the population that believes in life after death, this group actually grew in the United States between 1947 and 2001, while the percentage believing in an afterlife fell in most other postindustrial countries—from 68 to 47 percent in the Netherlands, for example.[29]

Taking these trends as a whole, we find it difficult to evaluate the extent to which religion is on the decline in the United States. One major challenge in making a general claim about the religious direction or trajectory of the US population is that there are so many different dimensions of religion (and therefore measures of it) to consider. Moreover, there is evidence that the decline in religious affiliation and involvement, especially over the past two decades, has primarily occurred among those who were only marginally involved initially. These loosely affiliated or involved persons are now more likely to report no religious affiliation or practice.[30] What is not clear is the extent to which this is a result of actual loss of belief and practice or of an increasing comfort in stating the absent or minimal role of religion in one's life to another person during a survey interview.[31]

Figure 1. Aggregate Religiosity Index (ARI), United States, 1952–2005. This figure shows the ARI for each year during this period. The scores are standardized to a mean of one hundred and a standard deviation of ten. The dotted lines show 95 percent confidence intervals based on bootstrapped standard errors. The index is republished with permission of Taylor & Francis Ltd, http://www.tandfonline.com, from J. Tobin Grant (2008), "Measuring Aggregate Religiosity in the United States, 1952–2005," published in *Sociological Spectrum* 28 (5): 460–76.

Another limitation to drawing broad conclusions about the historical trajectory of religion in the United States using GSS survey data is that these surveys only began in 1972, when all measures of religion reflected particularly high rates of religiousness. There is a temptation, then, to look at some of the downward trends, extrapolate backward, and assume that the farther back in time you go, the more religious the US population proves to be. For many, a religiously nostalgic view is tempting, but evidence from prior times suggests that today's levels of religiousness are not so different from the early 1900s or earlier and that the high religiousness of the 1950s may have been an anomaly. For example, Grant estimates a general level of religiousness for the United States from 1952 to 2005 using a measure of *aggregate religiosity* that draws on multiple data sources and dimensions of religion (see figure 1).[32] These methods produce evidence of a quite dramatic increase in religiousness from the early 1950s through the early 1960s.

Similarly, Finke and Stark merge a great deal of historical data on religious denominations and congregational or membership counts to demonstrate that the dynamics of religious institutions and membership started as far back as the 1700s.[33] They make a very compelling case for stability, if not for a boost in religious vitality, in the United States over time. Their assertion is that the rise in religiousness from colonial America into the future relies on the growth in numbers of religious institutions and memberships, and the documented higher increases in contexts that are seemingly more modern (e.g., urban areas) provide evidence that religion is not dying, especially not in relation to modernization.

Although some may believe that religion has been on the decline in the United States ever since the nation's founding, or that religiousness has remained unusually high and stable throughout US history, the truth is that religious patterns in the United States are complicated. Adding to the challenges of accurately characterizing the state of religion in America are key complexities underlying overall trends, such as diversity across demographic subgroups, changes in the demographic composition of the US population, the centrality of religious institutions (or congregations) in American religious life, and religion's historical role in defining and protecting social power and privilege in the United States. In this book, we clarify overall trends by revealing their components and drivers and by using three different lenses for understanding religion in America: the demographic, the congregational, and the historical.

A DEMOGRAPHIC PERSPECTIVE ON CHANGE IN AMERICAN RELIGION

The idea that religion is weakening in society is not just a popular news headline; it is also at the core of perhaps the longest-running and most contentious social theory of religion—secularization theory. Secularization theory has most often been discussed and applied in the contexts of the United States and Western Europe over the last century. There is much debate as to how exactly the theory is specified and what the best evidence is for testing the theory.[34] However, the language and ideas of secularization theory still very much dominate popular and scholarly discourse about the state of religion in society today. And, like it or not, the evidence brought to bear in these conversations usually involves trends in survey data comprised of individuals' self-reports of religious affiliation, practices, and beliefs. There are at least two problems with this approach. First, population-level trends can obfuscate different patterns of change for different subgroups in the population. Second, social changes, such as shifting levels of religiousness, are not only driven by people changing their beliefs and behaviors; they also result from changes in the composition of the population and changes in the size of subgroups. Thus, a fuller understanding of the state of religion in America over time requires attention to demographic processes underlying general trends.

A demographic perspective focuses on the composition of populations and how populations (and their components) change. Part of understanding a population involves understanding its demographics or the meaningful subgroups within it. When it comes to religion, we know that the experience and practice of it, in the United States and elsewhere, vary a great deal by demographics such as race/ethnicity, gender, and social class. Thus, it is important to follow differing trends across these various subgroups to know which ones might be driving certain forms of change or stability at the population level.

Furthermore, three key drivers of population change at large or within various demographic subgroups are births, deaths, and migration. Through these core processes, the age structure and other demographic features of a population can be altered. In addition, another set of demographic processes that results in population level change over time involves age, period, and cohort effects. Age effects refer to strong average patterns in how religious people are at various ages; period effects are when major events can trigger religious changes in everyone; and cohort effects come from people who were born about the same time living through a series of events at certain age points together, making their generation's life experiences and consequences uniquely influential on them in certain ways.[35]

Because the religiousness of certain demographic subgroups in the population (e.g., racial/ethnic groups, age groups, etc.) varies in all dimensions (e.g., affiliation, attendance, prayer, importance, etc.), change in the distribution of these groups in the population will shift levels of religiousness even if individual-level religious change is rare. Furthermore, new generations arrive on the scene and mature as older generations die, so if there is something different about how newer generations are religious (even if they remain stable over time), the loss of older generations will alter the religious makeup of the population through death without any conscious change among those who are living. For these reasons, it is important to think demographically about religion in the United States as a population phenomenon in addition to theorizing about why individuals may themselves experience religious changes (e.g., switching affiliations, attending religious services more or less often, or having their beliefs weaken) that aggregate up to the societal level.

Chapters 1, 2, and 3 of this book demonstrate the utility of a demographic perspective in understanding religious change. While the big picture trends in religion described above are often presented as if they represent overall changes for everyone in the United States, we show considerable diversity in how people from different racial and ethnic groups practice and experience religion in chapter 1. This chapter outlines differences in religious beliefs and behaviors for different racial/ethnic groups in the United States, including Black-White differences and Latinx American, Arab American, and Asian American distinctiveness. For example, there is a long-standing pattern of Black people being more religious than White people (on average), and there is considerable diversity in both religious affiliation and religious practices in different subgroups of Asian Americans. There are many explanations for these patterns, including historical exclusion and migration experiences (such as when and from which countries people migrate to the United States). We also document some of the ways that these differences between racial and ethnic groups have diverged or converged over the past few decades. In doing so, we break down simplified portraits of religious change in America to reveal distinctive trends for particular racial and ethnic subgroups in the United States.

In chapter 2, we dissect population trends in religion even further by considering gender and social class. Because race/ethnicity, gender, and social class serve as sources of both identity and social stratification, they intersect with religious identification and involvement in important and complex ways.[36] Many women's roles as mothers and their lower levels of labor force participation in earlier decades are two explanations for why women have historically been more religious than men. Likewise, the middle-class orientation of many religious communities often serves as a barrier to those with lower education and incomes, creating a gap in religious service attendance by social class. Paying attention to these structural complexities and how they combine enables us to think about even smaller and more specific subgroups, such as Black. college-educated women or White men with a high school degree, and to try to capture some level of intersectionality in relation to religious trends.[37] Additionally, the differences across these demographic subgroups provide contexts for understanding why changes in their size relative to other groups in the population (whether growing or shrinking) are important in any conversation about trends in religiousness in the United States. We tackle these issues of the varying composition of the US population and their role in religious change in chapter 3.

Chapter 3 discusses the core of what it means to study religion from a demographic perspective, and it outlines some of the key tools of demographic analysis: decomposing age, period, and cohort effects. We focus on questions like: Do people become more religious as they form families or as they grow older and ask tough questions about the afterlife? Do we see these changes over time in religion because there was some major event or change in the United States that resulted in lower levels of religious involvement? Or do we see a slight decline because each generation is less religious than their parents? These questions highlight the importance of studying trends in religion from each angle of age, period, and cohort, and the ways in which these trends can have overlapping effects. Then we present new analyses representing how population changes in fertility, mortality, and migration—three important fields of study for demographers—are related to religious change over time. We also examine what happens over time when social change and the resulting shifts in the composition of the population that are thought to influence levels of religiousness—such as increased educational attainment, delayed family formation, and an increasingly racially and ethnically diverse population—occur. These factors do not play as substantial a role as one might think in raising or lowering population levels of religiousness at this point, which indicates that American religion is somewhat resilient to other forms of social change.

In conjunction, these chapters demonstrate that the overarching, general population trends in religion in the United States often gloss over important variations across demographic groups and the impact that generational and compositional changes in the population can have regardless of whether any one American changes their religious beliefs or behaviors. Overemphasizing a slight overall trend of decline in religion over time ignores the vitality of religion within subpopulations such as Korean American immigrants. While some of these groups may only seem like small segments of the US population now, they are part of the shifting composition of the population, and paying attention to them helps us to recognize not only what the historic trends have been but also how these trends might change in the future as small groups become more significant portions of the population.

A CONGREGATIONAL FOCUS

It is important to remember that religion is not solely an individual activity but often takes place within groups and communities. Religious organizations and institutions represent another level at which we can study change over time in religious life in the United States. Congregations represent one of the most common forms of religious communities in the United States.[38]

In responding to secularization theory and its proponents, some sociologists point to the open marketplace of religious involvement in the United States in which new religious groups are continually being born, adapting, and dying.[39] Instead of these multiple religious options serving as a threat to religion, pluralism of religious groups instead contributes to the remarkable religious vitality of the United States.[40] There is some debate about the findings of these studies, but they provide a unique lens to observe issues at the heart of the secularization thesis.[41] They also establish the value in viewing American religion through an institutional or congregational lens.

As mentioned earlier in the introduction, the National Congregations Study (NCS) is a quantitative data source that allows us to track changes over time at the organizational level. Questions such as how many staff a congregation has, what is included in worship services, and what kinds of other activities the congregation engages in have opened up new realms of study in the sociology of religion. In addition, case studies of particular congregations, using interview and observational research methods, are a very useful tool for understanding these communities at a deeper level.

Since there are other books solely dedicated to changing trends for congregations, we devote just one chapter in this book, chapter 4, to highlighting two relevant trends for congregations: the increasing concentration of people in larger congregations, and the growing diversity across and within religious congregations. The trend toward increased concentration reflects the movement of individuals not only into megachurches—the largest congregations we tend to see and hear about most often—but also more broadly into larger congregations within each denomination. Multiracial or multiethnic congregations are one piece of growing diversity within congregations, as religious congregations are less likely to be fully White spaces and more likely to have some mixing of racial and ethnic groups.

Additionally, with the rise in the proportion of non-Whites and non-Christians in the United States, we have also seen greater variation in types of congregations, with more non-Christian worship spaces across the American religious landscape. Though occurring simultaneously, these trends have different implications: increased concentration gives greater power to the clergy who lead more members, while increased diversity suggests that congregations may represent one avenue toward restoring racial divisions in the United States.

Since a demographic perspective on religion demonstrates the importance that growing racial and ethnic diversity in the United States has for overall religious trends, thinking about how these trends might play out on an organizational level better captures what these trends might mean for the future of religion in America.

A HISTORICAL LENS

A third perspective we apply in this book for thinking about the state of religion in America is a historical lens. Doing so allows us to chart a broader history of religion in the United States in which we can situate trends of the past few decades. Apart from being a belief system that a person may hold or a community in which people can participate, religion also provides a set of values and beliefs that compete for primacy in society. Current debates over whether America is, or has ever been, a "Christian nation" are certainly not new, but they have been reinvigorated since the election of Donald Trump in 2016. For some, beliefs in Christian nationalism, or defending America's Christian heritage, were key drivers of support for Trump.[42] In an effort to trace these beliefs throughout the history of the United States, we broaden the focus to consider how religion in the United States, particularly White Protestant religion, has engaged in boundary-making processes throughout America's history. Doing so allows us to consider the contentious and often complex relationship between religion, politics, and social movements over time. These relationships are also closely related to the demographic changes happening within the US population, specifically the increases in immigration and in racial minority groups, described in chapter 3. As a result, while a historical approach utilizes different types of data and methods than a traditional demographic study does, highlighting both perspectives better reveals underlying components of religious change in the United States.

Chapter 5, our final chapter, adopts this historical perspective to consider how religion has been interwoven in American life over time and focuses particularly on the ways that religion has been used to build up and break down boundaries between different groups. We take a different approach from the other chapters, in terms of evidence, by citing the descriptions and comparisons of key historical events by other researchers. Building upon this work, we consider a thread running throughout much of US history: when religious and social or political groups or movements join forces, their doing so is often rooted in an effort to draw group boundaries to assert supremacy, usually ethnic or racial supremacy. Although key issues, alliances, and claims shift through time, religious, social, and political groups often ally with each other to claim societal power for themselves and restrict it for others.

FINAL THOUGHTS

This book contributes to conversations on the state of religion in the United States and how it has evolved over the past few decades by utilizing these three perspectives to capture religion in America in a deeper and more holistic way. Focusing on how trends vary by race, gender, social class, and other demographic categories, and on the role that age, period, and cohort processes play in changing levels of religiousness in the population helps us move beyond the limiting debate over whether Americans, as a whole, are more or less religious than they were five, ten, or fifty years ago and enables us to ask more interesting questions. Studying changes over time for religious institutions in the United States, as well as how religion and religiousness have shaped and been shaped by concerns over the state of America and a perceived loss of Christian values, helps us think about the importance of religion beyond the level of the individual. In doing so, we push back on the notion that religious change comes solely from individuals suddenly deciding to stop attending religious services or forgetting to pray. Rather, religious trends in the United States are interwoven with demographic processes affecting the population as a whole, changing institutions, and broader historical patterns.

In the conclusion, we return to these larger themes and reflect on the key claims of the book. We discuss the importance of the trends we demonstrate. We also look to the future, presenting evidence from studies projecting rates of religious belief, behavior, and belonging for the coming decades, and offering ideas for what will be important to follow and why.

Throughout the book we offer text boxes, graphics, figures, and tables that help illustrate key arguments presented in each chapter. The text boxes are designed to give you additional resources if you want to dig deeper on a particular topic, and they could be used as class activities or for your own independent learning opportunities. Many of the resources come from the Association of Religion Data Archives (ARDA), whose website provides an immense wealth of data and information.

1 Racial and Ethnic Variation in Religion and Its Trends

Observations about overall religiousness in the United States, and trends therein, mask a great deal of racial and ethnic heterogeneity in levels and types of religious affiliation, practice, belief, and commitment. Understanding religion in America requires careful attention to racial and ethnic differences, and an awareness of the history and size of various immigration streams. All Americans, except the few whose only ancestors were indigenous people, belong to family lines with histories of coming to America (by choice or force), of often bringing along religious practices and beliefs to share, and of adapting, in some ways, to the dominant religious cultures present upon arrival. In addition, there is a long history of exclusion of African, Latinx, Asian, Middle Eastern, or other racial or ethnic minority groups from predominantly White institutions, including religious communities. As a result, many groups forged their own religious paths, communities, and styles (again, by choice or force). There is a great deal of pride and a desire to maintain distinctions in many religious communities today. For all these reasons, understanding general patterns of religiousness in the United States over time requires the examination of racial and ethnic differences in the trends.

Furthermore, the racial/ethnic makeup of the US population has been shifting over time, contributing on its own to religious change in America.

If the proportion in the population of any particular ethnic group grows through immigration, and that group has higher or lower than average levels of religiousness, then its increased presence in the population will raise or lower overall levels of religiousness without any one person changing their beliefs or behaviors. For example, there is evidence that Central American immigration to the United States grew twenty-eight-fold between 1970 and 2018, and immigrants from Central American countries such as El Salvador and Guatemala have higher rates of religious service attendance in the United States than the general population.[1] It is likely that the rising numbers of US residents that have come from Central America, albeit still a rather small percentage, is slightly increasing the overall levels of religious service attendance in the United States. This may be offset by other groups of immigrants that are adding to the population but are less likely to attend religious services; however, the point is that it is important to understand the general differences in affiliation and practice across the main racial, ethnic, and immigrant groups in America. The intragroup trends over time present a more detailed picture of what religious change (or stability) in the United States looks like over time and for whom.

We use the terminology of "racial/ethnic groups" to represent a standard set of racial or ethnic categories commonly used in statistical analyses of the US population, such as Whites, Blacks, Latinx, and Asian Americans. These are large, oversimplified categories meant to approximate general differences in how people may or may not categorize themselves or others. Identifying with, or having others identify one with, a particular group shapes one's experiences, on average, given shared social backgrounds and experiences with and legacies of racism and xenophobia. We acknowledge that race is a social construct and that within larger racial and ethnic categories there is a great deal of heterogeneity in identities and experiences based on other factors such as one's country of birth, immigration experiences, physical characteristics, and the racial/ethnic composition of one's social networks.[2] Thus, we encourage caution in interpreting the patterns we present, keeping these limitations in measuring and interpreting racial/ethnic differences in mind.

In this chapter, we first present a review of what others have found regarding cross-sectional racial and ethnic differences in religious affiliation, practices, and beliefs. Many of these differences have held constant over decades, but they have not done so entirely, so we also use this chapter to examine the relatively minor yet interesting ways in which racial/ethnic disparities in religious practice have changed over time.

GENERAL RACIAL/ETHNIC DIFFERENCES IN RELIGIOUSNESS

Black-White Differences

Over four decades of data from national polls and surveys have demonstrated, on average, consistently higher levels of religiousness among Black Americans than White Americans.[3] Not only do Blacks have higher overall levels of religious service attendance,[4] many also spend over 50 percent more time at religious services each week than Whites: Black churches tend to hold longer worship services than predominantly White congregations.[5] Blacks are also *less* likely than members of other racial/ethnic groups to attend infrequently or never.[6] One study compared African Americans with European Americans, Latinx Americans, and Asian Americans and found that African Americans reported both greater importance of their faith in their lives and higher levels of belief that the Bible is the word of God.[7]

In terms of affiliation, African Americans tend to be Protestant and to identify more strongly with their religious affiliation; they also have a lower likelihood of being unaffiliated.[8] They are also more likely to join a voluntary association within the church.[9] This higher religious involvement of African Americans has been documented in multiple studies since the early 1970s and holds up even after analyses that control for other factors that could explain this pattern, such as differences in educational attainment, region of the country, and urban/rural residence.[10] In one study using seven data sets to test these Black-White differences, the only measures of religiousness that were not significantly different for Blacks and Whites were whether individuals received religious instruction growing up and their reported level of confidence in organized religion.[11]

Approximately 8 percent of Black US residents identify as Catholic, making up about 3 percent of the population of US Catholics in 2010.[12]

Early research on Black Catholics focused on the higher social status of African American Catholics as compared to other African Americans.[13] These scholars argued that African Americans converted to Catholicism because of both worship style preferences and a desire for social mobility or assimilation.[14] Other scholars have pushed back against this idea, finding that the majority of Catholics were second-generation and not simply seeking social mobility, as the pattern is less apparent among younger cohorts of African Americans.[15]

At an organizational level, predominantly Black Christian churches tend to vary from those that are primarily White in several ways. There are several historically Black Protestant denominations in the United States. These denominations emerged following emancipation in 1865 in response to both a desire for new churches among the newly freed population as well as the active exclusion of African Americans from the White churches that dominated the religious landscape.[16] Historically, Black churches provided far more than a weekly worship service, serving as one of the most important institutions for African American communities.[17] Though recent NCS reports suggest that on the whole African American churches are not more engaged in providing social services than other congregations,[18] other studies show they are more likely to provide particular social services, such as job-related and tutoring or mentoring programs.[19] This pattern applies to Catholic churches as well, since predominantly African American Catholic parishes are more likely than White parishes to engage in social service and social action programs.[20]

Lastly, churches in the predominantly Black Protestant denominations also have different worship styles, including more verbal affirmations and spontaneous physical worship. While verbal affirmation is common among White Pentecostal and other conservative Protestant congregations, spontaneous physical worship is far more distinctive to African American congregations.[21] In these ways, we see that religion intersects with race on the individual and organizational level: not only do Black and White religious people practice their religions in different ways; they also participate in organizations with differing styles and ministries.

We will return to common explanations for these differences by race after we outline the differences in religious affiliation, beliefs, and practices for other racial/ethnic groups in the United States. While Black-

White religious differences are discussed most often, other racial and ethnic groups have their own distinctive levels and forms of religious participation. Over the past few decades, as the size of other minority groups has grown, survey researchers have become better able to represent these populations in large, national data sets. Moreover, immigration is closely linked to many of these growing racial and ethnic subpopulations, so immigrant status and generation are also relevant to these discussions. We will return to the salience of the immigration experience and the variation by immigrant status after we describe the overall patterns.

Latinx Patterns

As of 2017, about 18 percent of the US population identify as Hispanic or Latino, making them the largest of all minority groups.[22] The Latinx population primarily identifies as Christian (77 percent total), including 48 percent who identify as Catholic. Summarizing these patterns another way, 34 percent of all US Catholics, 11 percent of all Evangelical Protestants, and 6 percent of all mainline Protestants are Latinx.[23]

According to national studies, Latinx Americans tend to express levels of religiousness that fall somewhere between those of Black and White Americans.[24] However, as is the case in any larger, panethnic category, there is variation across different Latinx subgroups. For example, Latinx Americans with Cuban and South American backgrounds tend to be less likely than other Latinx individuals to attend services weekly, while those with Central American and Mexican backgrounds are more likely to attend weekly.[25] Also, Latinx individuals who identify as Evangelical Protestants have higher levels of religious practice and are more likely to report that religion is important in their lives than Latinx Catholics.[26]

Asian American Variation

Asian Americans, as a group, tend to have the lowest levels of religious participation as compared to Whites, Blacks, and Latinxs.[27] However, there is considerable variation among Asian Americans by ethnicity, migration history, and social and economic background. For example, while 22 percent of the overall US population were unaffiliated with a religious denomination in 2016,[28] according to a survey from 2012, more than half of Chinese Americans were unaffiliated. In contrast, only about 10 percent of East Indian and Filipino Americans were unaffiliated.[29]

Since Asian Americans represent a small proportion of the US population (5.9 percent of the total population in 2018, according to Census Bureau estimates),[30] samples of Asian Americans are often too small to track change over time and variation by subgroups in large national surveys.[31] One pilot study found that 72 percent of Asian Americans have a religious identity, and they are more likely to be affiliated with a religious group than involved in other voluntary organizations.[32] Within the heterogeneous group we are referring to as Asian Americans there are varying patterns for different subgroups. Filipino Americans have the highest levels of religious identification and service attendance and Korean Americans have the second-highest levels. Chinese and Japanese Americans have the lowest levels of religious identification, which is likely the result of their concentration in secular areas such as the West Coast. Despite Christianity rarely being the dominant religion in Asian countries, it is the most common religious affiliation for Asian Americans. About one quarter of Asian Americans affiliate with a non-Christian religious tradition, including Buddhism, Hinduism, and Islam. Again, the diversity of this group produces variations in affiliation, as Vietnamese Americans are most likely to be Buddhist, and South Asian Americans are most likely to be Hindu.[33]

Religious diversity is evident among Chinese Americans given their long (but contentious) history of migration to the United States. Chinese Americans who have arrived since the immigration reforms of 1965 tend to be from urban areas in China and to have received a higher education prior to their migration, in contrast to earlier immigrants who came from rural areas in China.[34] Though almost half of Chinese Americans have no religious identification, their most common religious affiliation is Christianity, followed by Buddhism. Interestingly, many Chinese American Protestants converted from no religion to conservative Christianity in the United States.[35] Since the 1970s, there has also been some revival of Chinese folk religions through festivals and the reopening of joss houses, or worship spaces, which prioritize preserving Chinese culture.[36] Chinese American Buddhists have established temples that tend to be organizationally independent, and they often try to attract White, middle-class individuals to join their communities in order to integrate themselves in the community and enhance their American identity.[37]

One group that has received considerable scholarly attention are Christian Korean Americans. Korean immigrants tend to have high levels of religiousness, and some scholars argue that church participation is a way of life for Korean immigrants in the United States.[38] A large proportion of Koreans who migrate to the United States are Protestant because of the significant presence of Protestant missionaries in Korea. Additionally, Protestants in Korea tend to have greater socioeconomic status and therefore more resources enabling emigration.[39] Similar to other immigrant groups, Korean Protestants experience tensions over how to raise the second generation and whether or how to maintain the gender hierarchy from Korea in the United States.[40] In some cases, preserving a patriarchal structure in Korean Protestant churches reattributes social status to men that was lost owing to migration while excluding women from leadership roles.[41] In general, scholars also find that Protestant Korean Americans tend to be highly successful in passing down their religious beliefs to their children,[42] with almost two thirds of Korean American adults maintaining their childhood religious involvement.[43] However, this religious transmission may come at the cost of passing down other components of Korean history and ethnic identity, as parents often prioritize explicitly Protestant beliefs and practices and tend to exclude Korean folk traditions.[44]

It is important to keep in mind that the survey questions commonly used to measure religiousness in the United States tend to capture more Christian forms of worship (attending weekly services, praying, participating in small groups) that may not be as relevant for other religious traditions such as Buddhism or Chinese folk traditions.[45] As a result, we should be somewhat cautious when measuring religious participation and comparing groups that are not predominantly Christian to those that are.

Arab American Patterns

Overall, the Arab population in the United States remains relatively small at only 0.5 percent of the total US population between 2006 and 2010. But it is growing quickly and has increased by 76 percent since 1980.[46]

Moreover, the Arab American population receives a lot of attention because of geopolitical tensions involving the Middle East, the general population's unfounded assumption that those of Arab descent are largely Muslim, and the backlash against Islam in the United States since 9/11.

The US Census Bureau defines Arab Americans as those who trace their ancestry to seventeen Arabic-speaking countries in North Africa and western Asia. Over the last century, Arab Americans migrated to the United States in two distinct waves: a predominantly Christian wave from areas in what are now Lebanon, Syria, Palestine, and Israel; and a majority Muslim wave that came later. The foreign-born Arab American population is thus predominantly Muslim, but Muslims make up only about a quarter of the full Arab American population. Sixty-three percent of Arab Americans identify as Christian, and 13 percent identify as other or as having no affiliation.[47]

A survey conducted with Muslim and Christian Arab American women in 2000 revealed that Arab American Christian women are almost twice as likely as Arab American Muslim women to attend religious services at least monthly. On the other hand, Arab American Christian women are less likely than Arab American Muslim women to agree that religious scripture is the literal word of God.[48]

Despite their overall increase in the population, Arab Americans remain a small proportion of the total US population. Thus, it remains difficult to find reliable and representative survey data to characterize their religious beliefs and practices and to track changes in these practices over time. If the number of Arab Americans continues to grow, we expect future research to focus more on this ethnic group in order to compare them with other groups and to uncover the interesting diversity across ancestry groups and religions.

TRENDS OVER TIME IN RELIGIOUSNESS BY RACE IN AMERICA

Above we have summarized well-documented differences in religious expressions and experiences by racial and ethnic groups in America. The literature on this topic overwhelmingly focuses on absolute differences measured at one point in time, suggesting that racial/ethnic differences in religious affiliation, practice, or belief are relatively static. However, this is an open question. Have racial/ethnic differences in measures of religiousness changed over time? A big challenge to undertaking this investigation is the lack of good data. Although growing in number, most non-White racial/ethnic minority groups are small proportions of the overall population, so unless they are oversampled in survey studies, we often do not have the numbers to track trends reliably.

Additionally, the best survey for following long-term religious change in the United States, the GSS, was conducted exclusively in English until 2006 when a Spanish translation was added.[49] As a result, the proportion of Spanish-speaking Americans was likely underestimated in the GSS sample prior to 2006. Because the GSS currently only offers these two languages, Asian Americans are likely still undercounted in the GSS owing to language barriers, especially for recent immigrants. In addition to undercounting members of some racial/ethnic groups who do not speak English, the data collected from English speakers in these groups is likely biased toward those who have been in the United States longer, have higher socioeconomic status, or possess other sociodemographic characteristics correlated with speaking English fluently.[50]

Despite these limitations, the GSS data do permit us to look at racial differences in some trends over time, so here we examine race-specific trends in religious service attendance, prayer, and religious affiliation. The figures we present below are descriptive graphs plotting trends for two racial groups, Blacks and Whites. We do not control for any other variables in these results.

First, we consider trends in religious service attendance by race. Figure 2 presents rates of religious service attendance, or the probability of attending religious services in a given week.[51] In line with prior studies, we see the rate of religious service for Black Americans remains above that for White Americans across all five decades. Black religious service remains consistently just under a .5 probability of attending in a given week. White religious service attendance, on average, shows a more perceptible decrease, especially since the 1980s, when it began to drop from a probability of just over .4 to about .35. Thus, the racial gap in religious service attendance has widened over time owing to the persistent decline

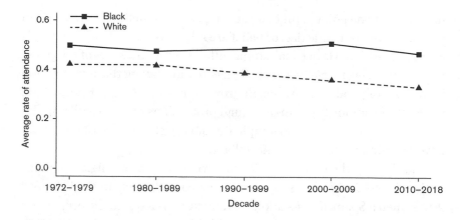

Figure 2. Rate of religious service attendance by race, United States, 1972–2018 (General Social Survey).

in the probability of Whites attending in a given week. The gap especially widened in the 1980s and 1990s when Black attendance appears to have been increasing while White attendance was decreasing. It remains to be seen how this racial gap will change going forward; however, in current discussions of the small but significant decline in religious service attendance in America we should be sure to remember that this trend is largely driven by the decreasing rate of religious service attendance among White Americans.

Figure 3 illustrates trends in rates of prayer by race, decade by decade, between 1983 and 2018. Again, not surprisingly, the probability of praying on a given day is consistently higher for Black Americans than White Americans. Comparing the trend lines, we see a slight widening in the gap owing to a small increase in the rate of prayer for Black Americans whereas the rate of prayer for White Americans has remained roughly the same. Our findings support the work of others that suggests little if any change in the frequency of prayer over time. Hidden in that general trend is a slight difference by race.

We also evaluated race differences in the most dramatic trend in American religion—the rise in number of those who report no religious affiliation. There was no difference in that trend over time by race. Black and White Americans, therefore, have been equally likely to indicate no

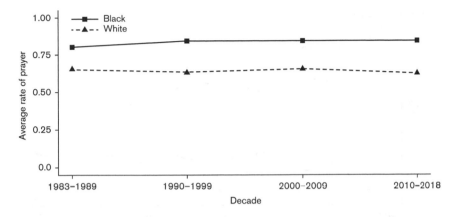

Figure 3. Rate of prayer by race, United States, 1983–2018 (General Social Survey).

religious affiliation over time, with both groups experiencing a dramatic increase in the religiously unaffiliated over the last two decades.

Splitting overall trends by race does not reveal dramatically different dynamics; but our results do suggest we should be careful to clarify for which groups religious change is happening and to what degree. In the next chapter, we go a step further and separate the population by race, gender, and education level to observe more interesting divergences in trends in American religion.

OTHER RACIAL/ETHNIC RELIGIOUS CHANGE

Some scholars have argued that the high proportions of Latinx Catholics migrating to the United States are helping to maintain the proportion of Catholics in the overall US population,[52] but it is important to keep in mind that not all immigrants from predominantly Catholic countries will identify as Catholic and be active participants in the Catholic Church.[53] Moreover, other scholars are starting to notice that high numbers of former Catholics are converting to Evangelical Protestant traditions or identifying as unaffiliated.[54] As a result, we are seeing high rates of former Catholics among the Latinx American population.[55] If this trend continues, we may begin to see declining rates of Catholics in the United States

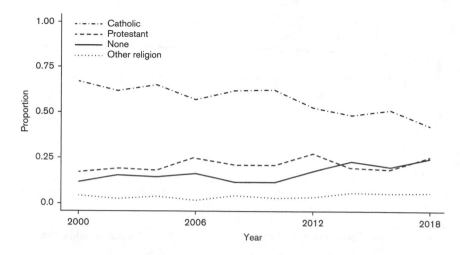

Figure 4. Trends in Latinx religious affiliation, United States, 2000–2018 (General Social Survey).

while the population of Latinx Evangelical Protestants grows. Latinx Protestants are likely to become an important demographic group given their significant growth and the diversity within this group.[56] Figure 4 shows some evidence of a recent Catholic decline and a Protestant increase using GSS data, but it is important to keep in mind that we can only distinguish those who identify as Latinx in the GSS since 2000. There is also a growing proportion of Latinx who do not report a religious affiliation. Tracking Latinx religious affiliation and participation over time will become increasingly important as this panethnic group continues to expand into a larger share of the US population.

The demographic composition of religious traditions has also changed over time. For example, we are seeing a convergence in educational attainment among different traditions, particularly Black Protestants gaining educational attainment closer to that of predominantly White religious traditions. While a majority of Black religious groups had very low average levels of education in 1990,[57] Black Protestants experienced a larger increase in average educational attainment than other religious traditions between 1972 and 1998; this is largely driven by cohort replacement.[58] However, Black Protestants are the most demographically distinctive group today, more so than White Evangelical Protestants, because they are disproportionately female with lower marriage rates and higher birth rates.[59]

Lastly, as the non-White population in the United States continues to grow, we would expect to see a growth in non-Christian groups. For example, the percentage of Black non-Latinxs who report a Muslim affiliation doubled between 2007 and 2014. While this doubling was a growth from only 1 percent of the population to 2 percent, it still suggests an important site of future research.[60] We have also seen increases in the political representation of other religious groups. Since 2007, Congress has included representatives who identify as Muslim, Hindu, and Buddhist.[61] The intersection of an increasingly non-White population with the racial patterns documented in this chapter will have interesting implications for our overall population trends in religion.

EXPLANATIONS FOR DIFFERENCES

There are many possible explanations for why levels of religious affiliation, practice, and belief vary by race and ethnicity. Some of these levels are common across groups and others are more particular to certain racial and ethnic groups. One theory often associated with African American religious distinctiveness but relevant for other racial/ethnic minority groups has to do with the link between religion and socioeconomic status. According to this theory, economic security is associated with feeling a sense of control over one's life, which can result in a lower need for religion to provide that sense of control.[62] By contrast, those who are more disadvantaged and marginalized in a society have less security, so they are thought to be more likely to be religious as well as less likely to disassociate from organized religion.

Alternatively, marginalized groups may also participate more in organized religion as a way both to resist and to cope with oppression.[63] Rather than simply being a response to insecurity, religious involvement can also be a conscious decision to affirm both individual and group agency over their marginalization and oppression. In these ways, we can see how religious involvement may be higher among groups experiencing this oppression and how this could apply to many of the non-White groups in the United States.

More specifically, the higher religious involvement of Blacks can be traced back to the long-lasting historical legacy of slavery and oppression. Indeed, as mentioned previously, all-Black religious traditions and denominations, sometimes referred to as the Black Church or African American Protestantism, emerged out of Reconstruction to serve a newly freed (but still restricted) population.[64] African American Protestantism is not particularly distinctive in its beliefs, but the strong emphasis on experiences, mystery, miracles, justice, and survival make up what some scholars call the five building blocks of African American Protestantism.[65] Believing that they have survived centuries of oppression and persistent discrimination in the United States only with the help and support of God is therefore fundamental to their higher religious practice as compared to other groups.[66]

Moreover, distinctive institutions and worship practices also contribute to higher religious practices among African Americans. Because Black churches were some of the first all-Black and Black-controlled institutions, their functions developed to serve the broader needs of their communities. As a result, Black churches were not simply worship centers; they also functioned as social service agencies, community centers, political organizing hubs, and even banks.[67] This combination of religious practice and social service is also expressed by distinctive worship styles that serve both those goals. Some worship styles, such as verbal affirmation and spontaneous physical worship, are often traced back even further to African religious rituals brought with slaves and modified to fit the American Protestant context.[68] These differences in worship styles are therefore a distinct product of a shared ethnic heritage and experience in the United States. Such widely shared worship components, specifically prayer and gospel music, are also tools that help to inspire and motivate community action.[69] In sum, the continued levels of higher political activism and community service activities among African Americans are the result of their distinctive religious traditions and institutions, and the continued importance of the Black Church in African American communities is one reason for the persistence of these differences between Blacks and Whites.

This greater religious involvement among African Americans may also reflect the theory that African American congregations, particularly in the rural South, represent a semi-involuntary institution.[70] Despite the contemporary emphasis on the voluntary nature of religious participation (people choosing their religious affiliation, switching if it does not suit them, or leaving when it no longer fits with their lifestyles),[71] social pressure within segregated Black communities in the South can drive participation among African Americans.[72] Tests of this theory have affirmed the overall idea of the Black Church in the South as a semi-involuntary institution, with the caveat that this pattern may apply to the South as a whole and not just the rural South. The rural South is distinctive for high levels of religious attendance across all denominations.[73]

Just as religion and race/ethnicity can intersect with immigrant status, so too can the experience of migration play a role in the varying levels of religious involvement by race/ethnicity. Both the kinds of religion immigrants bring with them and the ways they adjust to their new contexts have implications for their overall religiousness.[74] Migration can be a theologizing experience in which immigrants use religious consolation to ease the stress of leaving home and settling into a new environment.[75] For example, one explanation for the conversion of Chinese Americans from no religious affiliation to conservative Christianity is the desire for a religious framework to make sense of their premigration experiences in difficult environments and their experience as racial minorities in the United States.[76] However, migration can also be an alienating experience that disrupts religious practices as individual people become preoccupied with other demands, such as learning a new language and finding employment.[77] For many, religious institutions are a common source of integration and support for immigrants upon their arrival in the United States.[78] Because of this disruption, participating in religious communities, particularly ethnic communities, can help ease the transition.[79] It is important to keep in mind that not all immigrants will join a congregation in the United States, though, and the ones who join were in all likelihood more religious prior to their migration.[80] Additionally, those who affiliate with minority religious groups will have greater difficulty finding a religious community. For example, Hindus in the United States are likely to have fewer temples in their city than they did in India, which may lead to less communal participation and more personal practice.[81]

Many immigrant religious communities, regardless of religious tradition or country of origin, take to the institutional form of congregations in the United States in a process scholars call de facto congregationalism.[82] In many worshipping communities composed largely of immigrants, pastors and clergy members will adapt to meet the needs of their communities, providing tangible resources such as food, clothing, and legal counseling for immigrants while also helping them maintain their traditional customs.[83] Since religious organizations are an important source of social capital,[84] religious congregations are important places for immigrants to form connections with other people.[85] They also can serve as sites of empowerment for immigrant communities, since they provide free social spaces and religious networks.[86] In these ways, immigrant religious communities can function to promote social capital and social mobility.[87] Thus, higher levels of religious participation among recent immigrants, which are typically found among certain racial and ethnic groups, can partly result from the migration experience as well as the centrality of immigrant and ethnic places of worship to social life among many of these groups.

Historical factors and countries of origin also matter in explaining the variation in Asian American religiousness. While Chinese Americans often report no religious affiliation, they also have high rates of nonresponse to survey questions; this likely results from the ban on religion in China and their fear of persecution by the Chinese government.[88] Additionally, Japanese Americans were prohibited from practicing religion in Japanese internment camps in the United States during World War II, which likely contributed to their lower rates of religious involvement today.[89] One reason for the high religious involvement of Korean Americans is that Korean ethnic churches often serve not only as places of worship but also as educational centers, social hubs, and general welcome centers for newly arriving immigrants.[90] While predominantly Korean congregations can also function to maintain Korean traditions and customs,[91] Evangelical Korean churches tend to adopt more generic Evangelical characteristics and do not pass down these traditions to younger generations.[92] Additionally, most Koreans who migrate to the United States, particularly those from urban and middle-class backgrounds, have been exposed to Christianity prior to leaving Korea. Since Christianity in Korea is associated with westernized culture, Koreans who are familiar with Christianity and have the resources to migrate are more likely to do

Box 2 RACE AND RELIGION IN THE UNITED STATES:
A HISTORICAL PERSPECTIVE

As our chapter has documented, the racial and ethnic variations in religious life are closely interwoven with historical events and migration experiences. The Association of Religion Data Archives (ARDA) has created an interactive timeline to journey through many significant events in the United States related to race/ethnicity and religion.[1]

Through their learning module, you will be able to explore the role of religious groups in the abolition of slavery; when the first mosques, temples, and Sufi organizations were established; and key religious figures in the civil rights movement. This module fits well with this chapter while also setting you up for the narrative we describe in chapter 5—the power of religion to both unite groups and define social boundaries.

1 "Race/Ethnicity and Religion in American History," Association of Religion Data Archives, accessed January 20, 2020, http://www.thearda.com/learningcenter /modules/module42.asp.

so, contributing to the high levels of religious participation we see among multiple generations of Korean immigrants.[93] In these cases, we see the combination of historical factors, migration patterns, and demographic variables shaping religious diversity by race and ethnicity in the United States.

THE RACIALIZATION OF RELIGION

The widely renowned Black sociologist, W. E. B. Du Bois, observed in the early 1900s that religion was racialized, or that religion was more successful at reproducing racism and inequality than challenging it.[94] The Reverend Dr. Martin Luther King Jr. noted in an interview on *Meet the Press* in 1960 that eleven o'clock on Sunday mornings was the most racially segregated hour of the week in the United States.[95] A lot has changed since then, but eleven o'clock on Sunday mornings looks very similar today. Levels and types of religiousness vary by race, ethnicity, and immigration experience.

Studies operating from a lived religion perspective, or a focus on how religion is lived out in everyday life, teach us that religion is experienced and expressed differently based on the contexts in which we live and the identities we are negotiating.[96] With race, ethnicity, and immigration being such crucial parts of people's own histories as well as defining major social issues, there is no denying the importance of these characteristics in stratifying religious experience. Socially constructed racial and ethnic categories affect both how individuals think about themselves and how others label and treat them. Since religion is a personal and communal activity, racial and ethnic identities matter greatly in how individuals practice religion on their own and in communities. How racial and ethnic categories are constructed changes over time; tracking the link between religion and race/ethnicity over time is therefore an important task for demographers and social scientists. When studying American religion and its defining trends, we must be careful to discern when a trend is best understood by splitting apart groups to understand precisely where change is occurring and where it is not.

2 Complex Religion in America

Acknowledging and examining racial and ethnic differences in religious affiliation and practice, as we do in the previous chapter, is an essential step in more fully understanding the religious demography of the United States. Yet race and ethnicity, taken together, are but one kind of social stratifier or factor that can distinguish how we are raised, to what we are exposed, and the ways others will respond to us. All of these things impact our life options and outcomes. Social class and gender are also structures that refract religious identity and experience in unique and complex ways.[1] The expectations for and experiences of being religious (or not) are quite different for men, women, and those with other gender identities.[2] Studies also show that individuals' religious affiliations and behaviors are correlated with their level of education. This likely occurs through a reciprocal process whereby religious upbringings shape educational and career aspirations and achievements, and educational experiences and socioeconomic attainment influence subsequent religious behavior.[3]

As noted by Mary Jo Neitz, "religion is always gendered, as well as raced and classed."[4] Altogether and interactively, stratifying social institutions shape whether or how people practice religion and what they believe (or do not believe). Thus, it is imperative that we ask how religious patterns vary by key demographic subgroups and that we investigate how trends vary over time based on different combinations of social identities. So, how does religious affiliation or practice vary by social class and gender? Also, what have been the trends for Black men with higher education compared to White men with higher education or Black women with a high school degree or less compared to White women with a high school degree or less?

Building on the prior chapter's discussion of how levels and trends of religiousness vary by race, ethnicity, and immigration, we outline here over-all patterns, changing trends, and common explanations for the differences (or similarities) observed across social class and gender. Of course, race/ethnicity, class, and gender can never be fully disentangled from each other because they are intersecting identities in people's lives: the experience of life in one category often depends on the others. Thus, based on a simultaneous consideration of three important social identities—race/ethnicity, social class, and gender—we also demonstrate and discuss how religious trends in America vary. Since we discussed racial and ethnic differences extensively in the last chapter, we will pick up in this chapter with social class. After providing an overview of the differences in religious involvement by social class and gender, we move into a discussion of how race, class, and gender intersect with each other in complex ways to shape religious trends over time.

SOCIAL CLASS DIFFERENCES IN RELIGIOUSNESS

When it comes to differences in religious affiliation, practices, and beliefs by social class, patterns have remained relatively stable over time.[5] This is largely because of the ways religious practices have gradually adapted to fit with particular groups and communities. Researchers measure social class in various ways that include educational attainment, income, occupational status, wealth, or some combination of these. While the overall patterns are generally consistent across these measures, it is important to keep in mind that the theoretical explanations as to why religious involvement is tied to social class may also vary across different measures.

We can trace relatively consistent denominational social class hierarchies as far back as the colonial period of American history. As can be confirmed with data from as early as 1776 (and as recently as 2010), mainline Protestant denominations such as Episcopalians and Presbyterians have remained at the top of the social class distribution.[6] In fact, there was an overrepresentation of individuals affiliated with these denominations among the signers of the Declaration of Independence.[7] Using educational attainment, occupational prestige, and income, as well as more creative measures such as the number of business and political leaders from different religious traditions, we see that these groups have been found at the top of the distribution[8,9] White and Black Baptists have been consistently found at the bottom of the social class hierarchy, with mainline Protestant denominations falling somewhere in the middle.[10] Sectarian and more conservative Protestant groups are closer to the bottom of social class distributions, and they tend to be even farther down than their lower educational attainment would suggest.[11] In more recent decades, those who identify as Jewish have moved up the socioeconomic distribution and are now typically at the top of the distribution along with mainline Protestant groups.[12] The ordering of these denominations has remained relatively stable across both decades and recent cohorts, though we can see the overall increase in social status over time with a higher educational attainment of younger cohorts.[13] Even around the Great Recession, these stratification patterns remained largely consistent.[14]

Beyond these differences in religious affiliation, there are also differences in how people practice religion and what they believe according to social class. Those who rank their social class as "middle class" tend to have slightly higher rates of regular religious service attendance (as well as lower rates of nonattendance) than other classes.[15] However, those who identify as lower or working class report higher levels of belief in biblical literalism and in heaven and hell; they also more frequently report being "born again."[16] Lastly, there is less variation in frequency of prayer across social classes, though we see slightly higher rates of daily prayer in the lower classes and lower rates in the upper classes.[17]

Changing Trends

Though these patterns have remained stable, there have been some perceptible changes in the past few decades. For example, there has

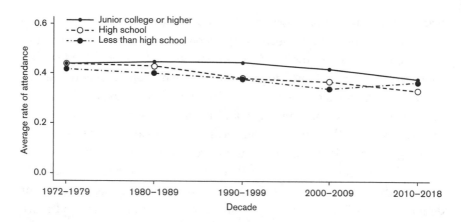

Figure 5. Weekly rate of religious service attendance by education level, United States, 1972–2018 (General Social Survey).

been some convergence in the average educational attainment across Protestant denominations. While the change has been slow, we are seeing some catching up of what were lower-strata denominations, such as Catholics and some Evangelical denominations, to higher-ranked ones like Episcopalians and Presbyterians.[18] This convergence is most evident in younger cohorts who experienced the expansion and greater accessibility to higher education and thus a broad increase in social status across all class groups, especially those with lower socioeconomic backgrounds.[19] Evangelical Protestants have also made significant inroads in terms of power and occupational status since the mid-1970s, building social networks and a highly public movement to increase their visibility and presence in elite and powerful circles.[20] Additional years of education are also associated with a higher likelihood of not affiliating with a religious tradition.[21] However, this association may have weakened over time.[22]

Figure 5 shows that having at least some college or higher education is related to a consistently higher probability of attending religious services in a given week.[23] Moreover, this education differential seems to have grown over time with rates of religious attendance falling slightly more quickly for the segments of the US population with a high school degree or less in education. The rise in average attendance for those with less

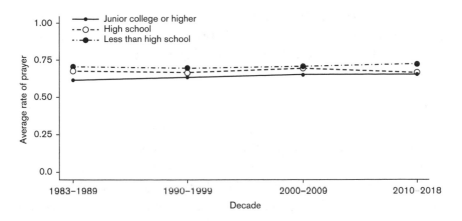

Figure 6. Daily rate of prayer by education level, United States, 1983–2018 (General Social Survey).

than a high school degree in the past eight years, which has nearly reached the level of those with some college or higher, is interesting, and time will tell whether this trend remains.

There are neither major educational differences in rates of prayer in the United States nor drastically different trends over time. Figure 6 charts the likelihood of prayer in a given day, and, as you can see, those with the most education (some college or higher) are the least likely to pray (although they still have a greater than .5 probability). However, it appears the education gap has been slightly shrinking, with a minor increase over time in the likelihood that those with some college education pray in a given day.

Moreover, as we saw in our discussion of religion and race/ethnicity in the prior chapter, the growth of non-White groups in the United States enables us to better capture the religious involvement of these groups in our large, national data sets and to test how it interacts with social class. For example, Hindus, Muslims, and Buddhists in the United States are near the top of the distribution in terms of both income and college educa-tion.[24] Furthermore, splitting up the large population of Catholics in the United States by ethnicity shows that there are social class variations within Catholics. While White Catholics have experienced upward mobil-ity in recent decades, Latinx Catholics rank lower than both Pentecostals and Black Protestants.[25] In this way, future research will need to investigate whether or how associations between social class and religious involvement vary by race, ethnicity, and religious tradition.

Explanations

The question of the link between social class and religion has vexed social scientists since the early days of sociology, with key figures such as Karl Marx and Max Weber having been part of this debate. A key challenge to understanding the linkage is that the effects can go in both directions—while social class can shape religious involvement, religious beliefs and affiliations can also shape social class. Both religion and social class are also passed down generationally, which means that in some cases this relationship can be traced across generations.[26] This link can be both advantageous and limiting. While some individuals are exposed to cultural and social capital that facilitate higher education and incomes, those who are not, or those who are exposed to cultural ideas and practices that work against social mobility, can be limited in their social advancement.[27]

More specifically, many scholars have identified elements of the cultural orientations religious groups provide that can hinder social mobility. An antagonism between some religious traditions and higher education institutions, which these religious groups see as having secularizing effects, has resulted in lower educational attainment for more fundamentalist, sectarian Protestant groups.[28] Students who believe in biblical inerrancy have lower GPAs and are less likely to take college prep courses.[29] There is also evidence that conservative Protestant women attend less selective colleges, despite having high academic ability.[30]

For similar reasons, these religious groups may also discourage wealth accumulation. Religious values pertaining to the belief that God owns everything can lead to an impulse to give money back to God through high levels of religious giving.[31] While conservative Protestant congregations and denominations often have a lower-class status because of the historical and generational factors mentioned previously, the religious values associated with them have the effect of further inhibiting their members' accumulation of wealth.[32]

Religious affiliation and involvement can also be correlated less directly with other demographic factors that are then associated with other forms of social status. For example, religion shapes people's goals and decisions regarding marriage and family formation in a way that can also shape educational attainment and accumulation of wealth.[33] The high value religious organizations tend to place on family formation results in earlier marriage and larger families for many religious young adults.[34] Then, early family formation is associated with lower educational attainment and financial earning.[35]

Similarly, religious participation also shapes people's social networks, which can be a key resource in social mobility.[36] Social networks can promote mobility by giving people greater access to resources and opportunities.[37] However, the stratification of religious denominations by social class limits the extent to which these connections can enable upward mobility for those with disadvantaged backgrounds, since religious participants largely interact with others like them in terms of race and social class.[38] One factor driving the stratification of religious denominations and congregations is that individuals' religious and worship preferences themselves may be directly shaped by their class backgrounds. As Nelson argues, middle-class individuals may be drawn to the trained choirs singing in Latin that are more common in middle- and upper-class Protestant churches; gospel choirs, however, appeal to those who prefer more familiar and participatory styles of worship.[39]

The last set of important factors driving the social class differences in religious involvement has to do with the barriers that can prevent working-class individuals from participating in religious communities. While lower-class individuals often report higher levels of commitment in terms of beliefs and prayer, they attend religious services less frequently. One barrier to religious service attendance for those who struggle to make ends meet is that congregations tend to be more welcoming of middle-class people, with working-class individuals and families not always feeling like they belong in those spaces.[40] Attending a weekly religious service also requires the resources of transportation, a work schedule that permits free time on Sunday mornings, good health, and minimal family demands.[41] Because these characteristics are likely correlated with social class as well, the barriers to religious participation can be steep for those who lack reliable transportation or are full-time caregivers.

Religion and social class are intertwined across the life course and have both independent and overlapping effects on other outcomes, creating a challenge for those trying to disentangle their effects. With the increased collection and use of longitudinal data, scholars will likely continue to investigate these phenomena using more advanced methods to better understand the relationships between religiousness and social class.

GENDER AND RELIGIOUSNESS

Looking at gender differences in religion, the pattern is rather basic: measured in multiple ways, women in the United States are more religious than men. This gender difference has existed through time and is found in many other societies.[42] American women are almost 10 percent more likely to report a strong affiliation with a denomination, to attend weekly religious services, and to have a certain belief in God without doubts. Women are also more than 25 percent more likely to pray daily than men.[43] These gender gaps are stronger for affective measures of religiousness, such as prayer and closeness to God.[44] As another measure of this religion gender gap, men are also more likely to have no religious affiliation than women.[45]

These gender patterns have not only been consistent over time and across different measures of religion; they have also been relatively comparable across religious traditions and countries. A recent Pew Research Center report not only found nearly universal gender gaps in religious involvement among Christian women; they also found that in none of the 192 countries for which they had data were men more than two percent more likely to be affiliated with a religious tradition than women.[46] When it comes to other more personal measures of religiousness, such as the importance of religion or the belief in heaven, hell, and angels, the Pew Research Center found little difference between men and women. Globally, there is also a smaller gap between Muslim men and women than between Christian men and women. One striking exception to the trends of higher female than male religiousness is that, among Muslims and Orthodox

Box 3 GENDER, RELIGIOSITY, AND YOUTH/
YOUNG ADULTS

While the main data source we use in this book is the General Social Survey, there are other surveys that focus specifically on youth. One study, the National Study of Youth and Religion (NSYR), surveyed and interviewed youth between the ages of thirteen and seventeen and followed the same set of youth until they were between the ages of eighteen and twenty-four. Interestingly, a gender gap is evident in this population, as well as on a variety of measures. The ARDA module on Boys, Girls, and Religion: How Adolescent Religiosity Differs by Gender allows you to explore the NSYR data for yourself to document the gender gap in attendance, views of religion, importance of religion, and other relevant measures.[1]

1 "Young Men, Young Women, and Religion: How Young Adult Religiosity Differs by Gender," Association of Religion Data Archives, accessed January 20, 2020, http:// www.thearda.com/learningcenter/modules/module23.asp.

Jews, men are more likely to attend religious services than women. This is largely the result of stricter norms for male attendance and participation in these traditions.[47]

Changing Trends in Gender and Religious Affiliation

Much of the existing research on gender differences in religiousness focuses on differences at one point in time or time-aggregated data, so we know less about if or how the gender gap in religiousness has changed in the United States over time. In figure 7, we break down the growing trend of being religiously unaffiliated by gender. As you can see, the increase in the proportion of the US population with no religious affiliation is growing slightly faster among men than among women. This has created an even wider gender gap in affiliation than during previous decades.

Turning to religious service attendance, the story is different. Here, in figure 8, we see both men and women follow the subtle yet consistent downturn in religious service attendance that others have observed for the

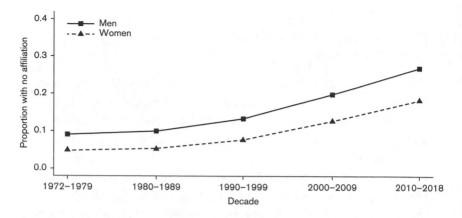

Figure 7. Proportion of population with no religious affiliation by gender, United States, 1972–2018 (General Social Survey).

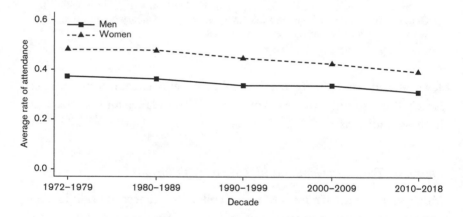

Figure 8. Weekly rate of religious service attendance by gender, United States, 1972–2018 (General Social Survey).

total population. Moreover, women are consistently more likely than men to attend in a given week. However, there has been a slightly steeper decline in the rate of religious service attendance for women than for men, so the gender gap in religious service attendance has been shrinking. This will be an interesting trend to follow. We also analyzed trends in rates of prayer and found very little change over time in the likelihood of individuals praying in a given day and, therefore, in the gender gap. Women regularly pray more than men.

Given the many changes in American women's lives over the past several decades, such as increased educational attainment and labor force participation, as well as delayed family formation, it is somewhat surprising that gender gaps in religiousness in the United States have not narrowed more. In fact, in some religious traditions, such as mainline Protestantism and Black Protestantism, women are becoming more of a majority.[48] We show that overall, men are increasingly more likely to be religiously unaffiliated than women.

Many scholars have predicted a convergence in men and women's religious service attendance resulting from women entering the workforce in greater numbers.[49] We similarly find evidence of women's attendance declining closer to rates of men's attendance,[50] but in Europe there has been more substantial convergence, and women are leaving religion altogether at a faster rate.[51] Still, in the United States and Europe women continue to be more likely to identify with a religion, to call themselves religious, and to participate in both public and private forms of religious involvement.[52]

Explanations

Scholars continue to debate the reasons for consistent gender differences in religiousness, and current research focuses particularly on different levels of risk aversion among men and women as an explanation.[53] Because religion offers a set of expectations for the afterlife, which is otherwise uncertain, believing and participating in religion serves as a protection against that uncertainty and minimizes risk.[54] The debate revolves around the question of whether these different levels of risk aversion stem from possibly biological differences or are the result of socialization.[55] Biological differences would likely mean that men and women are born with different levels of risk aversion, as well as other divergent personality traits that could also be related to avoiding risk. Socialization, by contrast, argues that women and men are socialized differently, with men receiving more encouragement for risky behaviors than women. While the exact sources of these differences remain unclear, risk aversion serves as one explanation for the gender gap in religious involvement.

Alternatively, another set of explanations focuses on the differences in what is expected of men and women in society. Since gender is socially constructed, men and women are constantly "doing gender" as well as "doing religion."[56] Because both femininity and religious involvement are associated with emotional expressiveness and submissiveness, women who are participating in religion are also "doing femininity."[57] Moreover, part of doing femininity also involves taking on family roles, such as the responsibility for the moral education of children in the household, so religion may fit more easily into female-typical family responsibilities.[58] In the same way, the historical pattern of lower work force participation for women also meant that in the past women would had more time to participate in religious communities and seek their social support.[59] Because women's labor force participation has grown and men increasingly help with family tasks, we might expect a convergence in men and women's religious involvement over time. We see that to some extent with religious service attendance. The fact that we do not see more of a convergence in levels of affiliation or personal practice, such as prayer, suggests, among other things, that societal norms and rewards for women being religious remain powerful.[60]

RELIGIOUS TRENDS AT THE INTERSECTIONS OF RACE, GENDER, AND EDUCATION

Although it may be insightful to parse trends in religion in the United States by demographic subgroups such as racial/ethnic groups, education levels, or genders, none of these individual social structures or identities operates in isolation from each other.[61] There is something unique about being a Black woman as opposed to being a Latina or a Black man, and Black women's experiences vary based on their education level, among other things. The lived religion perspective and ethnographic methods, or studying individuals as they live, are especially useful in discovering the ways that identities intersect to shape and be shaped by experiences. For example, in an ethnographic study of female prisoners and the primarily Black, middle-class, religious women who volunteer in prisons, Rachel Ellis shows that the actions and religious teachings of the volunteers are rooted in expressing femininity and godliness through the clothing and accessories they wore and through submission to a "good" man in marriage.[62] Much of what they encourage comes from their middle-class culture and is unattainable by women in prison who have nothing but prison-issued clothing. Some of the female prisoners have no interest in relationships with men, and those who do often return to communities with low employment and high incarceration rates. In sum, finding a "good" man is either undesirable or very difficult for these women. Ellis's research demonstrates how those with power in society end up defining boundaries around religious participation, and how those with other identities and experiences will therefore be less likely to engage.[63]

The idea that religious identity is in constant interaction with other identities has important implications for how we study religion and how we think about and measure religion's influence in daily life. Taking a lived religion perspective, which usually involves intensive, ethnographic case studies allowing for discovery of the ways in which people do religion outside the boundaries of religious institutions and balance multiple, sometimes conflicting, sets of beliefs, teaches us a great deal about how religion operates in America. In addition, the complex, interactive nature of religion calls for exploration of population-level religious trends at the intersection of various social structures. Findings from these types of quantitative analyses will by no means compete with the rich and insightful ethnographic work at the forefront of the lived religion and complex religion efforts. Instead, these intersectional trend analyses can serve as a complement to in-depth case studies. Quantitative analyses provide the advantage of being able to investigate trends over time for different subsections of the population, like whether gender gaps in religiousness are narrowing more among certain racial/ethnic groups or certain levels of social class than among others.

To do this, we create combinations of simplified indicators of race (Black or White), gender (female or male), and education (high school and less or some college and higher) and divide the General Social Survey respondents into eight groups (i.e., Black men who completed some college or more, White women who completed high school or less, etc.). We then chart trends in religious affiliation, religious service attendance, and prayer for these eight groups over time. We limit ourselves to these

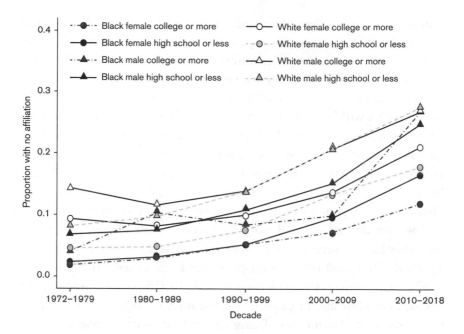

Figure 9. Proportion with no religious affiliation by combined race, education, and gender groups, United States, 1972–2018 (General Social Survey).

combinations in order to strike a balance between examining key intersections of social structure, having the sample sizes necessary to feel confident in comparisons, and keeping the analyses parsimonious. This results in the ability to consider some forms of complexity in religion over time; however, there remain many other investigations to be done for other racial/ethnic groups, other gender and sexual identities, other measures of social class, rural versus urban residence, and so on.

First, in figure 9, we examine changes in the proportion of individuals who have no religious affiliation for the eight intersectional groups. This reveals some complexity with regard to race, education, and gender. First, we see a convergence among White men in the two education groups. White men with some college education were previously more likely to have no religious affiliation than those with a high school degree or less. Now those two groups of White men are equally likely to be unaffiliated. There is some evidence that this same educational convergence has begun to occur among Black men as well, especially during the 2010s. This aligns with what some have identified as a growing deinstitutionalization of religion for lower socioeconomic groups; however, the results we present complicate that general trend somewhat.[64] This story is largely one about men, since it is less educated White and Black men who are showing the steepest increases in having no religious affiliation. We also note that college educated White and Black men have converged, both having very similar rates of being unaffiliated to men. Therefore, any alarm expressed about growing rates of religious deinstitutionalization among those with lower socioeconomic resources should be tempered by the acknowledgment that this is no more likely to occur than what has been going on among college-educated men for decades.

The story is different for women. For a few decades, White women with high and low education levels also seemed to be converging in terms of the likelihood of their not having a religious affiliation (less educated women were catching up to women with at least some college education). However, more recently, it is White women with some college education for whom the proportion with no religious affiliation is growing the fastest. They are the group closest to reaching the same level of having no religious affiliation as men. The gap between college-educated White women and White women with a high school degree or less is now widening. We also see a widening of the education gap for Black women, but in a reverse manner. For Black women, the less educated are showing more growth in having no religious affiliation than those with at least some college education. In fact, the group that has consistently remained the most likely to be religiously affiliated is more highly educated Black women. Studies have shown that Black adolescents from socioeconomically disadvantaged backgrounds often rely on religious institutions to keep them focused on their education.[65] Therefore, Black women who have been to college may have benefitted from religious institutions in a way that keeps them more affiliated across their life course than others. Moreover, any narrowing of the racial gap in religious affiliation in the United States owes more to Black men's changing levels of affiliation than Black women's. The less dramatic increase in non-affiliation for Black women with some college education is slowing what has otherwise been a dramatic rise in having no religious affiliation in the United States.

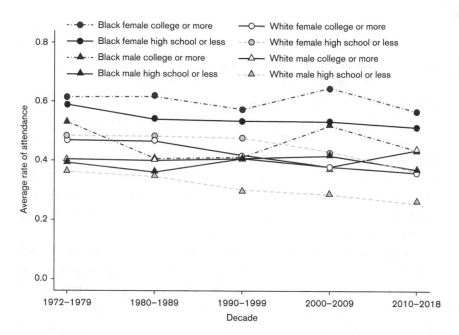

Figure 10. Average rates of religious service attendance by combined race, education, and gender groups, United States, 1972–2018 (General Social Survey).

Turning to religious service attendance, we see in figure 10 trends broken down by our eight groups of intersecting identities. The results are quite revealing. First, not surprisingly, Black women are consistently most likely to have attended religious services, hovering between a .5 and a .6 probability of attendance in a given week. In general, in the years between 1972 and 2010, any declines in religious service attendance largely came from White men and women; rates of Black religious service attendance are rather stable. In the 2010s we have seen the most consistent decline across all groups, so this is certainly a trend to keep our eyes on; however, the long-running, small-but-perceptible decline in religious service attendance in the United States noted by multiple scholars and mentioned in the introduction, is largely a story about declines in religious participation for White Americans.[66]

The gender and education patterns among White Americans are very interesting. White women (with any level of education) have converged to a

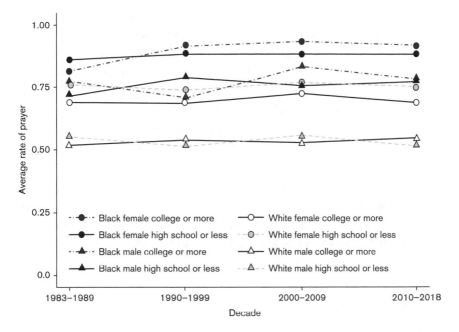

Figure 11. Average rates of prayer by combined race, education, and gender groups, United States, 1983–2018 (General Social Survey).

similar rate of attendance as White men, averaging lower attendance than White men with some college education and higher attendance than White men with no college education. In other words, the gender gap in attendance would have disappeared if it were not for White men with no college education, whose rate of religious service attendance was among the lowest in the 1970s but fell even farther away from other groups to a probability of about .25 that they would attend religious services in a given week. White men with no college education are becoming increasingly disconnected from religious congregations in the United States. This fuels the gender gap and, to some extent, the overall decline, in White religious service attendance.

Examining rates of prayer over time by the eight intersectional groups charted in figure 11 shows, first and foremost, a relative stability in prayer for all groups across four decades. If anything, there appear to be a slight increase in prayer for Black women and men and a slight decrease in prayer for White women and men. These trends then counteract each other when looking at average prayer rates for the entire population where scholars have found long-term stability.[67] There appears to be no convergence in gender prayer gaps except possibly among college-educated Whites in the 2010s. The most striking thing about this figure might be what is missing compared to our analyses of religious affiliation and religious service attendance, and that is a distancing of White men with lower education levels. Their rates of prayer, although among the lowest at about .5, have remained steadier than their rates of religious affiliation and religious service attendance. This provides more evidence that White men with lower socioeconomic resources are experiencing a deinstitutionalization of their religious lives. They may pray at about the same rate, or at least report praying at the same rate, but they are increasingly unlikely to be religiously affiliated or to attend religious services.

FINAL THOUGHTS

Religion is expressed and experienced differently for different subgroups in the population. Social class seems to sort Americans into different religions or denominations (and vice versa), and the standard gender gaps in different measures of religion appear to hold in the US population. However, taking race, education, and gender into account simultaneously, we see some interesting dynamics. Black, highly educated women remain distinctively religious across time, and White men without a college education seem to be driving the overall trends observed for the population as a whole: the growing proportion of Americans with no religious affiliation and the recent decline in frequency of religious service attendance.

There are, of course, important qualifiers and caveats to the patterns we have presented here. First, these figures present averages, so while people's racial/ethnic, social class, and gender identities are not determinative of how they will be religiously, these factors are related to population-level patterns. Thus, it is possible that you or others you know have experiences counter to these averages. In those cases, it is likely that other social structures are at play. For example, it is likely that sexual orientation, political identity, one's status as a recent or second-generation immigrant, or one's place of residence interact with race/ethnicity, class, and gender to shape religious patterns. In some of these cases, we are limited in terms of available data. For example, many nationally representative surveys lack the sample sizes to assess trends and make comparisons for LGBTQ individuals, although other research suggests we should pay further attention to their religious patterns.[68] Also, at some point, it is too complicated to quantitatively combine and have so many variables interact at once. Finally, as noted previously, the standard categories used to classify race/ethnicity, social class, and gender are not always as neatly separated in reality as they are in the statistical models researchers use.

It is important to recognize the limitations of our approach and the types of analyses reviewed and presented here, but there is great value in revealing part of the complexity in overall population trends in religion in America. When you hear social pundits discuss the increasing number of Americans without a religious affiliation or the decline in religious service attendance, you can now process this information with the understanding that this is not the case for all Americans, and that religious change (and stability) in America is often limited to certain social strata.

Another layer of complexity in considering how religion varies across social strata is that often these social groups are changing in size across time, which makes their contributions to levels of overall religiousness in the population rise or fall. For example, as higher education becomes more common in the population, or as the proportion of non-Whites in the United States increases, the trends for highly educated individuals and non-White Americans can become more important in shaping the overall population trend. In the next chapter, we turn to considering how the population of the United States changes over time in size and composition, and how these demographic changes play a role in the religious trends we observe.

3 A Demographic Perspective on Religious Change

Public conversations about religious change in society often focus on what is thought to make individuals become less (or more) religious. Is it a loss of morals? Is it a loss of respect for religious leaders? Is it the way religion and politics are becoming intertwined? At the heart of these proposals for explaining religious trends is an assumption that religious change in society comes from individuals consciously changing their religious beliefs or practices. Changing levels of religiousness, whether decreasing or increasing, are often envisioned as sea changes brought on by large-scale social change or events that lead people to become less (or sometimes more) religious.

Social changes that occur in a specific period of time and influence entire populations (i.e., people of all ages) at once are what demographers call period effects.[1] There are two other types of population-level social change—age effects and cohort effects—that also provide valuable insights into how and why average levels of religious affiliation, practice, or belief in America might rise or fall even if no single American changes anything about her own religiousness over time. Although less frequently invoked in conversations about why society has or has not changed religiously, age and cohort processes, together with period change, are important and

56

understanding them gives us a fuller picture of how levels of religiousness in society change (or not) and in what direction.

PERIOD EFFECTS IN AMERICAN RELIGION

Social scientists contend that cultural shifts in recent decades have contributed to large-scale religious change during particular periods of time (period effects). In their book on religion in America, Robert Putnam and David Campbell argue there have been three "seismic shocks" that have shaped religious life in the United States.[2] First, the 1960s was a time of questioning authority. Political protest was visible and widespread. It was a very active era for the women's movement, the civil rights movement, and antiwar demonstrations. During this time, religion, as an authority structure, was not immune. Religious observance dropped. Wuthnow argues that this era led to a shift from a dwelling, or an institutionally-based, form of spirituality, toward a seeking or less conventional form of spirituality that can operate outside of religious institutions.[3]

As a second major period change in religiousness in the United States, Putnam and Campbell argue that the revitalization of religious practice and the rise of Evangelicalism and the Religious Right from the 1970s to the 1980s was a reaction to the turbulence of the 1960s. Wuthnow asserts that in the period following the 1960s, self-help and therapy became more common, and Americans sought a return of stability from a more or less fictionalized past.[4] This seeking style of spirituality encouraged individuals to develop their spiritual lives in the ways that worked best for them. For example, many individuals integrated secular forms of self-help with the services that religious congregations also developed to meet these needs. In this way, Wuthnow argues, Americans experienced a cultural shift in how they engaged with spirituality.[5]

The third shock to religiousness in America that Putnam and Campbell describe involves the growing number of individuals moving away from organized religion, beginning in the 1990s, as a reaction to the increasing alignment of conservative Christianity and politics.[6] Wuthnow notes that this bifurcation took place even earlier; he argues that the denominational organization of religious institutions gives way to special interest groups like the Moral Majority, Christian Voice, Religious Roundtable, and the National Christian Action Council.[7] These groups (especially Evangelicals) revitalize religious participation by amplifying fear of secular change and link it to political identification and values. Much of the recent surge in having no religious affiliation comes from the growing frustration political liberals and moderates have over the active and conservative politicization of many American religious organizations.[8] At this point, it seems like this political backlash will continue to drive liberals and moderates away from organized religion. However, recent scholars have posited that if more liberal politicians were to embrace narratives about America's past, present, and future offered by more theologically and politically progressive religious groups, politically liberal or moderate individuals might not so quickly give up on organized religion.[9]

AGE OR LIFE CYCLE CHANGE IN RELIGIOUSNESS

When it comes to social change, age effects (sometimes referred to as life cycle effects) refer to a set of relatively predictable changes that occur in the course of many people's lives and when they are roughly the same age. These age effects happen with regularity across generations, though with some variations in the exact timing of the changes. Age effects can stem from physiological change, psychological development, social role or status changes, or a combination of any of these.[10]

The most prevalent forms of age-related religious change include higher levels of religious involvement in childhood, when parenting school-aged children, and in retirement.[11] Lower average levels of religious involvement tend to occur in mid-to-late adolescence and young adulthood, when parents become empty nesters, and at the end of life when one's health and mobility decline.[12] These age effects occur not only in the United States but around the world, with the strongest age patterns in Western countries.[13]

Why might these age-related changes in religiousness persist generation after generation? Scholars suggest social and transcendental reasons. Parents with young children and people in older age groups are often looking for social support from religious institutions, and people at a similar life stage are often easily found within religious institutions.[14] Religious institutions also provide social gatherings or programs—such as family nights, mothers' groups, men and women's groups, or retreats—that bring people in similar social roles and age ranges together.[15] Often, those in retirement get involved in volunteer opportunities through religious institutions.[16] These opportunities provide a sense of shared belonging and experience.

Another way that life cycle or age effects persist across generations involves the commonly understood idea that religion can deliver key transcendent resources at critical points in the life course. For example, some may look to a higher power for strength and inspiration to be a better parent or to a religious tradition to have a moral system to pass along to their children. Some may draw upon religious ideology to understand and cope with health challenges in old age or the idea of one's mortality.[17]

In sum, across all generations, year after year, there remain age-related factors that affect the likelihood of someone being religiously affiliated, attending religious services regularly, praying, or practicing other aspects of religiousness. We must be aware of these dynamics when we are looking for generational change in religion. If we take data from one point in time and compare a younger age group or generation to an older age group or generation, we might assume that those differences are generational in nature. In fact, these differences might be age related. When trying to gauge generational differences in religion, it is important to compare different generations' levels of religiousness at certain common age points. For example, the next time you read in the media that a younger generation is less religious than those who came before, check to see whether the data analysis accounted for age effects. In other words, the two generations should be compared to each other at similar age points (e.g., using data collected when each group's members were between the ages of twenty and twenty-four). Otherwise, the differences observed could be explained by the tendency of young people from all eras to be less religious during that phase of life as compared to others rather than by some kind of generational decline.

Finally, we must also consider that when the age structure of a society changes, the average level of religiousness in a society can change, making it seem like there has been an overall secularization or sacralization when really it is one age group and its typical level of religiousness (whether higher or lower) contributing more to the population mean than before. For example, the baby boomer generation, born between 1946 and 1964, was an unusually large cohort, so part of the slight, general boost in religiousness in the United States in the 1980s and 1990s could have been owing to the fact that baby boomers were raising young children during a phase of their lives often characterized by higher religiousness, on average, thus increasing population-level estimates of religiousness. In other words, individual baby boomers may not have been behaving any more or less religiously than most adults during that phase of their lives, but they were, overall, a larger cohort and therefore contributed more to the calculation of the population mean, raising overall religiousness during those decades. Another aspect of age structure that can change average levels of religiousness is when life expectancy is improved and people in a society live longer. We know that older people tend to be more religious than younger people, so if people in older age groups live longer and make up a larger proportion of the overall population than in the past, their typical levels of religiousness will factor in more and raise overall religiousness.

COHORT OR GENERATIONAL RELIGIOUS CHANGE

The other demographic source of social change that can explain why average levels of religiousness in the population rise or fall is cohort change. Birth cohorts are groups of people born around the same time; such cohorts are also known as generations. Cohorts can be defined by any range of birth years. In demographic analyses, you will often see one-, five-, or ten-year birth cohorts (e.g., individuals born in 1980, 1980–84, or 1980–89). Sometimes analysts will rely on socially-defined and named generations, such as baby boomers, Generation X, or millennials.

Birth cohort change comes about because those born in a similar era experience the same historical events and social contexts at the same ages.[18] For example, consider the Great Depression of the 1930s in the United States. Many people faced severe economic deprivation then, but the impact the Depression had varied depending on people's ages. For example, very young children might not remember anything about the

Box 4 COHORT VS. GENERATION

What is the difference between a cohort and a generation, and what is the value in one over the other? Researchers use the concept of a cohort as a group of people who have a demographic experience in common (e.g., they are born within a year, five years, or ten years of each other). A cohort, or set of cohorts, is well defined, and if time distinctions are being made, they are generally uniform across groups. Generations, on the other hand, are less precisely bounded by time. They usually refer to a group born around the same time, and they are often named and characterized in a way that combines a variety of features. They tend to take on a life of their own, and, being more cleverly titled, are more memorable.

The Pew Research Center, which is an extraordinarily useful resource when it comes to information on social trends and includes a very strong subdivision for *Religion & Public Life*, sometimes reports their findings by generational groups. In an article on their website, Michael Dimock explains how they define the generations they use.[1]

As somewhat of a counterpoint, in a blog post on *Family Inequality*, Philip Cohen discusses the problems that can arise when using these popular generations as comparison groups.[2]

1 Dimock 2019.
2 Cohen 2014.

Depression and be less affected by memories of it, but adolescent girls at the time often had to take on a large share of the domestic responsibilities so their mothers could work outside the home and help provide for the family. Both the mothers' and the adolescent daughters' cohorts would then be uniquely influenced (one getting experience in the labor force and the other becoming more independent and perhaps specialists in domestic work).[19] Similar kinds of arguments can be made for how various historical events, experienced at certain points in the life course, may be more influential on a certain cohort's religious characteristics.

For example, while the increasing link between conservative religion and politics is at least partly a period effect (i.e., it seems to be happening across all cohorts in some fashion), it has had different implications for different cohorts. As mentioned earlier, many argue that the higher rates of having no affiliation among younger cohorts is partly a backlash against having grown up in the era of the politically active Religious Right.[20] Those in younger cohorts who feel only a weak connection to religion and are more liberal are more likely to reject religious involvement and affiliation because of religion's increasing association with conservative politics. In this way, a period effect also resulted in a generational change.

Scholars have identified numerous differences in how cohorts engage with religion and spirituality. Many scholars have examined the religious and spiritual lives of the baby boomer generation, owing to that generation's numerical dominance.[21] Because of the tumultuous nature of the 1960s and 1970s, the period effects documented here had a significant influence on the cohort that came of age during the 1960s. In one in-depth analysis of this cohort, Roof found that baby boomers were distinctive in their quest culture focused on self-fulfillment and the multiple sources from which they built their religious and spiritual practices. As they rebelled and pushed back against other institutions during the 1960s, many also left their religious institutions, opting for more individualized and personal forms of religious involvement.[22]

Cohorts born after the baby boomer generation have also developed their own distinctive patterns of religious involvement as a result of their experience with changing social trends. Examining individuals between the ages of twenty-one and forty-five from 1998 to 2002, Wuthnow provides a context for understanding the declining numbers of young adults active in religious organizations. The key trends facing this cohort include delayed marriage and childbearing; having fewer children; facing high uncertainty in work and finances; and loosening community relationships. Because marriage, childbearing, job stability, and commitment to communities have all been shown to increase religious involvement, the postponement or absence of these things in the lives of young adults has important implications for their religious involvement.[23] Cohort changes can also shape how closely some of these variables are associated with religion, though. While higher education has typically been associated with a greater likelihood of not affiliating with a religious tradition, this effect appears to be declining across younger cohorts, such that in younger cohorts, people with college degrees are more likely to affiliate with a religious tradition than those without a degree.[24]

The clearest evidence for cohort effects on religion in America is in the form of a phenomenon called cohort replacement. This occurs when each new cohort tends to have lower levels of some characteristic, such as religious involvement, so that as the oldest generation dies off, the average level of religious involvement across the whole population automatically gets lower and lower. Furthermore, as the members of each new generation are less likely to be raised in religious households (because fewer parents are religiously affiliated), they are also less likely to raise their children in religious households, perpetuating these cohort effects over time.[25]

Scholars have generally attributed the slow decline in religiousness over the last half century to cohort replacement.[26] Evidence for cohort replacement has been shown in declining religious service attendance, religious affiliation, frequency of prayer, and belief in biblical inerrancy.[27] Moreover, these cohort replacement patterns in the United States are similar to those of other Western countries including the United Kingdom and Canada.[28] There are, however, some exceptions to patterns of religious decline across cohorts. Some scholars have observed an increase in belief in life after death across younger cohorts in Europe and a stability in this regard in the United States.[29]

All in all, though, while there is evidence of cohort replacement playing a role in changing levels of religiousness, cohort changes have been very small. It has taken decades to detect significant movement. However, with recent evidence for stronger intergenerational transmission of having no religious affiliation, this trend could accelerate among future generations.[30]

PUTTING IT ALL TOGETHER

To provide a concrete, visual demonstration of how to think about age, period, and cohort change, we created table 2. This table shows the percentage of GSS respondents who are religiously unaffiliated every ten years, starting in 1976, and broken down by ten-year age groups. To evaluate

Table 2   Percentage not affiliated with any religion by age group and survey year, United States, 1976–2016 (General Social Survey)

Age Group	Survey Year				
	1976 (%)	1986 (%)	1996 (%)	2006 (%)	2016 (%)
20–29	13	10	20	24	36
30–39	9	9	11	22	33
40–49	4	8	14	14	22
50–59	2	4	7	15	17
60–69	4	2	5	10	16
70+	3	2	5	7	11

age-related religious change, we can look row by row down each column to see the differences in affiliation rates across age groups. For example, if we look at the first column, we can compare each row to the next one down and ask whether, in general, twentysomethings are more likely to be unaffiliated than thirtysomethings; how thirtysomethings compare to fortysomethings; and so on. As you can see by looking down each column, the percentage of people with no religious affiliation tends, with only a few exceptions, to decrease with age. In general, across time and cohort, older Americans are less likely to be religiously unaffiliated.

To evaluate cohort change in the percentage of people with no religious affiliation, we can focus on each full diagonal of cells and how they compare to the diagonal next to them (another cohort). If we start in the most upper-left cell of the table, we see a group of twenty- to twenty-nine-year-olds in 1976 of whom about 13 percent reported no religious affiliation. Then we can follow the cells from that top left corner down to the bottom right corner and see that when the same cohort (those born between 1947 and 1956) was sixty to sixty-nine years old, about 16 percent reported no religious affiliation. By comparison, a slightly older cohort of people, born between 1937 and 1946 (aged thirty to thirty-nine in 1976), started off with lower percentages reporting no religious affiliation (9 percent), and only increased to 11 percent by the time they were seventy or older. A cohort slightly younger than the initial cohort started at lower levels of those reporting no religious affiliation (10 percent) but experienced a larger increase over time to 17 percent reporting no religious affiliation in 2016. In other words, it seems that for the cohorts in this table that provide us four or five decades of data, each new cohort experiences a greater increase in the percentage of religiously unaffiliated people across their lifespans.

Earlier we discussed the increasing proportions of those who report no religious affiliation in each new or younger cohort. We see this pattern by comparing different cohorts at a common age range or by looking across a single row. While only 13 percent of those who were twenty to twenty-nine years old in 1976 reported no religious affiliation, this jumped to 36 percent of twenty- to twenty-nine-year-olds in 2016. Even in the older ages where we see lower proportions reporting no religious affiliation, we see a difference between only 4 percent of those in their sixties in 1976 reporting no religious affiliation, as compared to 16 percent of those in their sixties in 2016. As members of these older cohorts pass away, the percentage of those in the whole population with no affiliation shifts more and more toward the (higher) percentages seen in younger cohorts. This is the process of cohort replacement.

Finally, we can use table 2 to look for evidence of period change. The question is, do all cohorts experience the same level of change in one decade? If the answer is yes, we would expect to see a similar change in each cohort-diagonal (comparing one cell to the next cell down and over) for all groups. This would tell us that something happened to the population as a whole in that decade. In other words, young adults, middle-aged adults, and older adults all increased or decreased in their affiliation rates at a similar magnitude over a particular decade. So, for example, between 1976 and 1986, those who started between twenty and twenty-nine years old and aged up to thirty to thirty-nine years old saw a decrease from 13 percent to 9 percent in the number of those that were religiously unaffiliated. To capture period change, we want to see if all the other age groups experienced the same level of change between 1976 and 1986. In this case, the amount of change was very different for each cohort. For example, the cohorts that were forty to forty-nine or fifty to fifty-nine in 1976 showed no change in the percentage of the religiously unaffiliated (those percentages remained at 4 percent and 2 percent, respectively). So, there is no evidence of uniform change across all groups over this entire time period.

Of course, a more precise examination of period effects requires methods designed to control for age and cohort variation, but in this simple descriptive table there does not appear to be much evidence for period change except for some similarities across cohorts between 1996 and 2006. If we take the level of not having a religious affiliation for each cohort in 1996 and compare it to that cohort's level in 2006 (move one cell to the right and one cell down to find a cohort's level in the next decade), all age groups seem to experience between an increase of 1 and 3 percent of those who are religiously unaffiliated. For example, the birth cohort comprised of people aged twenty to twenty-nine in 1996 went from 20 to 22 percent unaffiliated; the cohort comprised of people aged thirty to thirty-nine in 1996 went from 11 to 14 percent unaffiliated; and so on. These small but consistent increases in the percentage of cohorts with no religious affiliation between 1996 and 2006 suggest there may have been some across-the-board period change in religious affiliation during that decade. However, we do not see a similar pattern when comparing other decades.

Hopefully, these numbers help demonstrate how to think about variations in religiousness that can come from (1) changes in a population's age structure that shift the balance of the population in more or less religious phases of life (age effects); (2) overall changes in the whole population (period change); or (3) changes that come from the unique experiences and birth or death of each new generation (cohort effects). It is very difficult to estimate the proportions of observed trends in religiousness that are attributable to each type of variation, because age, period, and cohort are linearly related (for example, if you take the year and subtract a person's age, you will know their birth cohort).[31] Complex statistical methods exist to work around this challenge and produce reliable estimates.

Using one of these complex approaches to study age, period, and cohort patterns of nonaffiliation, Schwadel finds support for a lot of what table 2 suggests. He finds evidence for period change, with overall increases (regardless of age or cohort) in the percentage of people with no affiliation between the 1990s and 2006 (the last year of data he analyzed). He also finds across-cohort increases in the percentage of people with no religious affiliation starting with those born in the 1940s.[32] In other work, Schwadel finds evidence for across-cohort declines in religious service attendance, the belief in biblical literalism, and prayer, but he also finds that belief in an afterlife is stable across time and cohorts.[33] This mirrors the conclusions of Voas and Chaves, who argue that cohort replacement is driving much of the slow but steady decline in religious affiliation, attendance, and belief in God.[34]

Another study with a more global focus was conducted by Hayward and Krause, who used World Values Survey data to examine time trends in eighty countries between 1981 and 2013.[35] They found persistent age effects in most societies, with old age being associated with higher levels of religiousness (although this varied in magnitude across societies with especially strong age effects in Western nations). They found period effects in many regions, but these effects were very heterogenous in direction and magnitude. These period changes were often related to national wealth, with increases in it leading to declines in religiousness. Cohort change was only significant in a few countries, so Hayward and Krause concluded that general aging processes and material well-being are mostly related to religious change around the world, but that the speed and nature of these processes vary greatly across cultures.

As you can see, there is still a fair amount of debate over which demographic processes are more influential in religious change. In the United States, however, it does seem that evidence increasingly supports the slow process of cohort change as a factor in the growing category of having no religious affiliation and the slight decline in religious service attendance. It remains to be seen whether the effects of cohort replacement will be ongoing and whether some forms of religious belief and more personal religious practices will follow this pattern as well.

SHIFTING DEMOGRAPHIC COMPOSITION AND RELIGIOUS CHANGE

Another way that populations change over time is in their demographic composition or in the relative size of various demographic subgroups. Three demographic rates crucial to the size and age composition of populations are birth rates, death rates, and migration rates; however, there have been few empirical analyses designed to examine how various fluctuations in these rates, and therefore in the demographic composition of the United States, have accelerated or suppressed religious change. To address these gaps, we review expectations for how a changing population might influence average rates of religiousness, and we present a set of descriptive analyses testing whether societal-level modifications in fertility, mortality, migration, education, and employment have contributed to, or buffered, changes in rates of religious affiliation, religious service attendance, and prayer.

When it comes to population-level fertility, an increase in birth rates will tilt the age distribution of a population toward younger ages, and improvements in life expectancy (or decreases in mortality rates) will tip the population toward older ages. Because of the age effects on religious change, when a population has more younger adults than older adults contributing to a measure of average religiousness in the population, it will be less religious on average. However, during periods of higher fertility, adults spend more years of their lives as parents of young children, and that tends to raise religious involvement.[36] Therefore, when birth rates are higher and adults are more likely to have young children in their homes, the average level of religiousness in the nation will be higher as well. Of course, fertility also contributes to religious change by determining how many offspring are eligible to become a new generation of followers. Fertility has been shown to be very important for religious population growth in the long run.[37]

At the other end of the life course, in old age, when retirement might free up more time for religious involvement or proximity to death might raise the attention given to spiritual matters, religiousness is generally higher.[38] Hence, when a population's proportion of older members increases, average religiousness in the full population will rise.

Migration is another population phenomenon likely to affect the religiousness of a population. In the United States and Western Europe, some recent streams of immigration have introduced more highly religious (on average) groups of people to the population, thus raising overall religiousness.[39] Furthermore, increases in the proportion of the population identifying as racial/ethnic minorities through immigration and higher fertility of native minority groups is also likely to raise average religiousness, because African Americans, Latinx Americans, and other racial/ethnic groups are on average more religious than Whites.[40] However, as noted in chapter 1, migration can also disrupt religious practices for newly arriving immigrants, so not all immigrants maintain their religious affiliation and behaviors in the United States.[41]

While international migration to the United States can affect overall levels of religiousness, internal migration, or people moving to new cities or states within the United States, can also have implications for trends in religiousness. This is also called residential mobility (moving to a new place) or residential stability (staying in the same place); there are multiple hypotheses for how changing rates of mobility affect religious affiliations and practices. The United States, which is typically seen as a country with relatively high residential mobility as compared to other countries around the world, has seen declining rates of mobility over the last three or four decades.[42] This trend is the result, broadly, of changing demographics in the population (an aging population and shifting household structures), economic shifts, and changes in technology.[43] For example, improved communication technologies and transportation enable people to work from home, giving them the opportunity to stay in the same place and commute longer distances as needed rather than moving for a job change.

In terms of how these trends affect religion, the patterns are less clear. One hypothesis is that mobility is disruptive for religious involvement. Strong social ties and social integration increase religious participation, so losing these relationships as a result of moving to a new city can reduce religious service attendance.[44] However, there is also a chance that losing people's social ties increases religious participation in their new homes as they seek to form new relationships.[45] Alternatively, moving can create a "revolving door" or a "circulation of saints" in which trends in religious attendance are net zero as people leave one religious community and then join another.[46] In terms of affiliation, mobility can result in switching to new denominations as a result of regional variation in religious traditions.[47] Residential mobility can also be related to the age effects we described above when moves are associated with particular life stages, such as moving out of one's parents' home after finishing high school or college; moving to a new place to start a first job; or moving following marriage or divorce.[48]

Since the empirical evidence provides greater support for the hypothesis of increased mobility reducing religious involvement, the declining rates of residential mobility in the United States across this time period could be buffering against a steeper decline in religiousness.[49]

Over the last several decades the United States has experienced dramatic changes in education. The percentage of adults in the United States over age twenty-five with at least some college education grew from 10 percent in 1940 to 60 percent in 2016. The percentage of men and women over age twenty-five with some college education was even (10 percent) in 1940, but in 2016, 62 percent of women and 59 percent of men over age twenty-five had some college education; so, women's increases have been slightly greater than men's.[50] Although many believe that higher education is secularizing, in fact, studies show that educational attainment is positively associated with religious affiliation and participation for both men and women.[51] Therefore, the rising average education of the population is likely working to keep average levels of religiousness higher in the United States.

Rates of labor force participation grew rapidly for women (ages twenty-five to fifty-four) from the 1970s to a peak of 77 percent in 1999, hovering around that through 2015.[52] For men between the ages of twenty-five and fifty-four, by contrast, there has been a slow decline in labor force participation, from a peak of 97 percent in the mid-1950s to about 88 percent in 2015.[53] Research suggests that when it comes to income, high-earning men are more likely to be religiously involved than low-earning men, but high-earning women are less likely to be religiously involved than low-earning women.[54] Therefore, perhaps the lower rates of employment for men and the higher rates of labor force participation for women will both contribute to lower average religiousness in the United States over time.

CHANGING DEMOGRAPHICS AND RELIGIOUS AFFILIATION

In the introduction to this book, we summarized trends in the percentage of the population belonging to different religious groups or denominations, particularly highlighting the recent and substantial increase in the percentage of Americans who report no religious affiliation. Here we ask the question, how might the change in the distribution of religious groups between 1977 and 2018 have been different if certain shifts in the demographic composition of the American population had not occurred? In other words, if we weight or adjust the 2018 GSS sample to have the same proportion of individuals with certain demographic characteristics as 1977 (e.g., the percentage having a preteen child in the home), how would that alter the level of religious change experienced?[55]

All analyses presented in the remainder of this chapter are provided separately by gender. This is because many of the demographic characteristics we are examining have changed in substantially different ways for men and women, with implications for how these changes then relate to religion outcomes. For example, women have achieved greater gains in education and full-time employment over these four decades than men, so we feel it important to model these processes separately. In fact, some of the compositional changes may vary considerably across racial or ethnic groups or across levels of education, and as the previous chapter showed, there are important intersections in race, gender, and education level. Because we find gender to be one of the most distinguishing variables for the processes discussed here, we limit our analysis to differences by gender. However, future research should pay attention to the ways that the composition of subgroups has varied over time and contributed to their unique trajectories.

In figures 12 (for women) and 13 (for men), the first (or farthest left) two bars show the actual distribution of the population across religious affiliations in 1977 and 2018, respectively. Comparing these two bars with each other shows how the percentage of the population identifying with each religious group (or none) has shifted in four decades. Here we see a dramatic increase in those with no religious affiliation; some growth in non- Judeo-Christian faiths and female Evangelical Protestants; some contraction among Catholics, Black Protestants, and male Evangelical Protestants and Jews and a large decline for mainline Protestants in their share of the US population.

Working to the right of the first two bars, the rest of the bars show what the 2018 distribution of various religious categories *would* have been if certain features of the demographic composition of the US population

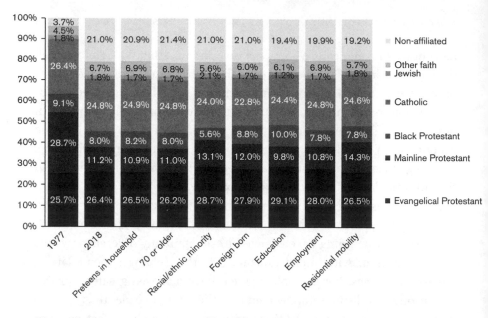

Figure 12. Percentage of women affiliated with religious traditions in 1977, 2018, and predicted levels in 2018 if demographic characteristic shown remained at 1977 levels, United States (General Social Survey).

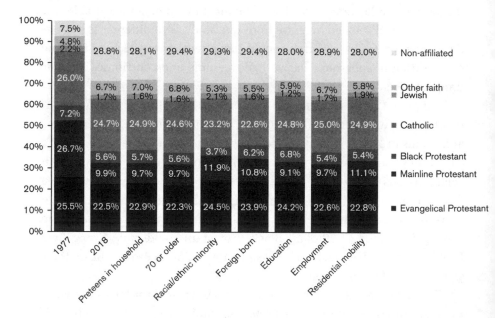

Figure 13. Percentage of men affiliated with religious traditions in 1977, 2018, and predicted levels in 2018 if demographic characteristic shown remained at 1977 levels, United States (General Social Survey).

had not changed since 1977. This gives us a general sense of the role some shifts in the demographic composition of the US population have played in the growth or contraction in various religious groups. As you can see in these figures, variations in the demographic composition of the United States played a very small part, if any, in the overall distribution of religious groups between 1977 and 2018. Population fluctuation is typically slow, but if change continues in the same direction and over many years, the long-term contributions of some changing demographics may still play a key role in religious change.

Looking at the top section of all the bars in figures 12 and 13, we can evaluate how the dramatic increase in those with no religious affiliation between 1977 and 2018 might be related to some aspects of demographic change. What we see for women in figure 12 is that if women's education, labor force participation, and geographic mobility would not have increased between 1977 and 2018, there would have been slightly less of an increase in the percentage of women reporting no religious affiliation by 2018. In other words, a small part of the increase in the percentage of the female population that has no religious affiliation may come from the fact that more highly educated women, women working more hours, and women who do not live close to where they were born are more likely to not have a religious affiliation. For men, these demographic changes do not seem to be as related to the rise in the unaffiliated. On a very small level, without changes in fertility and divorce related to the chances of having a preteen in the home, increases in men's education levels, or changes in residential mobility patterns, there may not have been as much of a rise in the group of religiously unaffiliated men. On the other hand, without the aging of the population and the growing racial and ethnic diversity and immigration, we would have seen even more men identifying as unaffiliated.

Looking at the second category in each bar, we see the proportion of the US population who affiliate with a religion falling outside of the other categories we have included in the figures (this group includes Buddhists, Hindus, Muslims, and others). Between 1977 and 2018, this part of the population grew from just over 4 to more than 6 percent of the population. For both men and women, as expected, if the US population had not become more racially and ethnically diverse owing to increased immigration to the

United States, there would not have been as much of an increase in those affiliated with religions other than Christianity and Judaism. Because immigrants from the last several decades have come from countries with more diverse religious backgrounds, we have seen some growth in this very segment of the US population.

Jewish people make up a very small percentage of the population—1.8 percent of women in 1977 and 2018 and 2.2 to 1.7 percent of men across those same years. There is some indication that for women, the proportion of those who identify as Jewish may have somewhat increased were it not for growing racial and ethnic diversity in the population and may have declined if education levels for women had not increased during this same period. For men, there may have not been a notable decrease if racial and ethnic diversity had not increased between 1977 and 2018 and there may have been more of a decrease (to 1.2 percent) if male education levels had not increased. Because most people who identify as Jewish also identify as White, when racial/ethnic diversity increases, the proportion of Jewish people in the US population will shrink, even if no Jewish individuals change their affiliation.

Now to a larger religious group in the United States—Catholics. Diversity and immigration, as expected, play a role here, but not as big of a role as we might expect. The percentage of the US population identifying as Catholic stayed relatively stable from 1977 to 2018, dropping only 1.6 percent for women and 1.3 percent for men. And although many attribute the stabilization of the Catholic population to immigration from Latin American countries, and higher fertility among these immigrants in the United States, our analysis suggests these have not been major factors. If the percentage of the population in racial/ethnic minority groups or those who are foreign born had stayed at the same level as in 1977, the decrease in the percentage of Catholics between 1977 and 2016 would have been 1 or 2 percent more, for both women and men.[56]

The percentage of the US population who affiliate with a historically Black Protestant denomination declined a little more than 1 percent from 1977 to 2018, and our analyses suggest this stability is in large part owing to the growing racial diversity of the United States. If the racial composition of the population had stayed the same as it was in 1977, we estimate the percentage of the population affiliated with Black Protestant groups would have fallen to 5.6 percent for women and 3.7 percent for men.

The second most dramatic change in the distribution of religious groups in the United States between 1977 and 2018 is the decline of mainline Protestants from 28.7 percent to 11.2 percent of the population for women and from 26.7 percent to 9.9 percent for men. This decline could have been slightly curbed if the proportion of the population in racial and ethnic minority groups had not grown as much and residential mobility had not declined over this time period. On the other hand, their presence in the population would have dropped even lower, to 9.8 percent for women and 9.1 percent for men, if education rates had not risen in these decades.

The proportion of the population who identify with Evangelical Protestant denominations went up slightly for women (25.7 to 26.4 percent) and down for men (25.5 to 22.5 percent). Interestingly, we find that the ratio of the women with an Evangelical Protestant affiliation may have been 2 or 3 percent higher if the racial/ethnic population had not diversified as much since 1977. Also, for women, it seems the Evangelical Protestant share of the population would have grown more if immigration and women's education and employment rates had not increased. For men, racial/ethnic minority and immigrant increases in the population in addition to their rising levels of education contributed somewhat to their decreasing proportion in the population.

In sum, we see some small role for all of these demographic changes in fueling or offsetting some changes in the size of certain religious groups over time. Fertility, mortality, and migration, all of which relate to the changing size of racial and ethnic groups, and the changes in rates of education and employment have served to alter the religious demography of the United States over the course of the past four decades.

COMPOSITIONAL CHANGE AND RELIGIOUS SERVICE ATTENDANCE

We now turn to the question of how rates of religious service attendance shifted between 1977 and 2018 and the role of the changing demographics of the US population. The first two rows of numbers in table 3 display the change in the rate of religious service attendance, for women and men, between 1977 and 2018. You might remember from chapter 1 that these rates can be interpreted as the probability of attending a religious service in a particular week: for example, someone who reports attending services nearly every week would have a probability close to one; while someone who reports never attending would have a probability close to zero.[57] Women start with a higher probability of attending in a given week and decrease to a probability that is still higher than the probability for men. Then, in each row below those estimates, we calculate what the probability of attending religious services in a given week in 2018 would have been if one demographic change between 1977 and 2018 had not occurred. In other words, we hold these demographic characteristics constant at the 1977 level. So, for example, if American adults had the same probability of having a preteen child in their homes in 2018 as they did in 1977, the women's rate of religious service attendance would have dropped to .385 rather than .382 and the men's rate would have only dropped to .315 compared to .308. As we mentioned earlier, the likelihood of having a preteen child in one's household has fallen over time, owing to lower fertility in general, higher nonmarital fertility, and divorce. And because having younger, school-aged children is highly predictive of religious service attendance, when people have fewer children and there are fewer co-resident parents of young children, the proportion of the population most likely to be attending religious services regularly is lower.

Next we look at what the 2018 rate of attendance would have been had life expectancy not increased. If we kept the percentage of the population living past seventy years of age constant at 1977 rates, the probability of attending religious services would have dropped more for women (to .379) and men (to .304). Thus, increases in life expectancy over the past four decades have somewhat offset what might have been steeper declines in religious service attendance.

Growing racial and ethnic diversity has also played a role in offsetting declines in religious service attendance. Keeping the proportion of the population who identify with a racial/ethnic minority group constant at 1977 levels would have led to even more of a decrease in the frequency in religious service attendance. So, part of what has kept the United States more religious, in terms of religious service attendance, is the changing racial and ethnic composition of the population. There is no statistically

Table 3 Predicted change over time in probability of religious service attendance in a given week if certain demographic changes had not occurred, United States, 1977–2018 (General Social Survey)

	Probability of Attending Religious Services in a Week	
	WOMEN	MEN
1977	.497	.365
2018	.382	.308

2018 probability, if changes below had not occurred since 1977:

Decreasing likelihood of having a preteen child in the home	.385*	.315*
Increasing likelihood of living past age 70	.379*	.304*
Growing racial and ethnic diversity of the population	.373*	.303*
Increasing number of foreign immigrants	.379	.305
Increasing educational attainment	.372	.296*
Increasing employment for women, decreasing for men	.390*	.304
Decreasing rates of geographic mobility	.382	.306

* Statistically significant (p < .05) contribution to or offsetting of change over time in attendance, estimated with Oaxaca-Blinder decomposition analysis using linear regression.

significant difference in the 2018 rates of attendance and what a model holding immigration levels constant at those of 1977 would predict. Thus, despite what many often claim, it does not seem like the growing immigrant population is raising rates of religious service attendance. This supports findings that suggest some streams of immigration bring more religiously active people to the United States and some bring less religiously active people.[58] With the two streams counteracting each other, the growing immigrant population would not have an effect on religious service attendance levels in the United States.

The remaining variables also do not appear to contribute significantly to change and, with two exceptions, they show minimal differences in comparison to the 2018 attendance rates. Had female employment rates not increased, there would not have been as much of a decline in religious service attendance among women. Likewise, without the increase in male educational attainment, there would have been a greater decline in religious service attendance among men.

COMPOSITION OF THE POPULATION AND CHANGES IN PRAYER

We also use GSS data to look at the role of demographic change in shifts of the frequency of prayer over the last four decades (see table 4). The first two rows of numbers reveal change between 1977 and 2018 in rates of prayer first for women and then for men. Women were more likely to pray in a given day than men at both time points, but while women have experienced a small drop in the likelihood of their praying daily, the probability for men has increased slightly. These changes are much smaller in magnitude as compared to the changes in religious affiliation and attendance rates, so the roles of individual population shifts are much less noticeable for prayer rates.

Now, looking at what would have happened if various demographic changes had not happened, we see that the only statistically significant factors for both men and women are the aging of the population and the increasing proportion of racial and ethnic minorities in the population. If there had not been an increase in the proportion of the population aged seventy and over since 1977, the probability of praying in a day would have dropped slightly lower by 2018 for both women and men. And if there had not been an increase in the proportion of the population that identifies with a minority racial/ethnic group, there would have been an additional, sizeable decline in the probability of praying in a given day between 1977 and 2018. There is one other factor at play for women, which is that if the proportion of women who are fully employed had not increased since 1977, their probability of praying in a given day would have only dropped by .02 rather than by .05. Though small, the change that has occurred is partly the result of changes in the demographic composition of the US population, the most important of which

Table 4   Predicted change over time in probability of praying in a given day
if certain demographic changes had not occurred, United States,
1977–2018 (General Social Survey)

		Probability of Praying in a Day	
		WOMEN	MEN
	1977	.760	.558
	2018	.755	.566

2018 probability, if changes below had not occurred since 1977:

	WOMEN	MEN
Decreasing likelihood of having a preteen child in the home	.755	.568
Increasing likelihood of living past age 70	.753*	.562*
Growing racial and ethnic diversity of the population	.748*	.551*
Increasing number of foreign immigrants	.757	.564
Increasing educational attainment	.769	.574
Increasing employment for women, decreasing for men	.758*	.560
Decreasing rates of geographic mobility	.755	.566

* Statistically significant (p < .05) contribution to or offsetting of change over time in attendance, estimated with Oaxaca-Blinder decomposition analysis using linear regression.

seem to be attributable to aging, growing diversity, and women's increasing education.

DEMOGRAPHIC MOMENTUM AND LIKELY RELIGIOUS CHANGE

This chapter shows how a variety of demographic processes have altered the composition of the population, resulting in admittedly subtle but interesting adjustments in average levels of religiousness in the population. Some of this change happens regardless of whether individuals themselves change their religious affiliations, rates of religious service attendance, or the frequency at which they pray. Therefore, trends in religiousness in the United States and other societies should be thought of as reflective both of aggregated, individual-level variation in religion in a society and of the changing demographic composition of who is living in that society at any point in time (and how demographic characteristics are correlated with religious affiliation, attendance, or prayer).

Population composition shifts are small and therefore very slow across time, except in the case of widespread death or migrations owing to wars or epidemics. This means that this type of change is unlikely to produce radical shifts in religiousness in a population. Furthermore, the demographic changes that have occurred have been in a variety of directions, which means that some changes render others unnoticeable. Regardless of their small magnitude, demographic changes carry momentum. The United States is likely to continue to experience lower fertility rates. Changes in life expectancy have slowed but could pick back up with medical advances, especially if tragically high mortality rates among lower socioeconomic groups and African Americans are reduced.

The increasing racial/ethnic diversity of the US population between 1977 and 2018 seems to have played a key role in overall religious change in the United States. In chapter 1, we discussed how religious affiliation, attendance, and prayer, among other aspects of religiousness, vary by race and ethnicity; this explains why a greater share of the population identifying as Black, Latinx, or another racial/ethnic minority group weights the total population toward higher levels of religiousness. Given current political realities, the future of immigration to the United States and other countries is uncertain, but whatever direction it takes, immigration will continue to shape the religious character of societies in interesting ways.[59]

If anything, it seems surprising that certain demographic alterations have not sparked a more noticeable change in the religiousness of the population. Many have assumed that the dramatic alterations in women and men's lives and family formation and structure over the past few decades would have contributed to substantial religious change. Instead, it seems that religious individuals and institutions may have found ways to adapt that have prevented population-level changes in education, employment, and fertility from greatly altering the religious landscape. In the next chapter, we discuss changes over time for religious congregations, so we invite you to consider how the population-level changes discussed here may also be driving changes at the institutional and organizational levels of religion.

PREDICTING THE FUTURE

Demographic principles and data can also be used to project future trends in religiousness based on expected population change in coming decades. For example, Skirbekk, Kaufmann, and Goujon rely on estimated differences in fertility, migration, intergenerational religious transmission, and switching among eleven ethnoreligious groups to predict future trends in the United States. They project that Hispanic Catholics will grow rapidly as a proportion of the US population between 2003 and 2043 (from 10 to 18 percent), and that mainline Protestants will continue to decline.[60] They predict that immigration will continue to increase the percentage of Hindu and Muslim residents in the United States while lower fertility will contribute to a decline of the already small Jewish proportion of the US population. Hackett and other scholars use over 2,500 data sources to make similar projections worldwide. They project that the percentage of the world's population who are religiously unaffiliated will have declined from 16.4 percent in 2010 to 13.2 percent in 2050. This is because, worldwide, those without a religious affiliation are having fewer children than the religiously affiliated, so the increasing number of people who switch from having a religious affiliation to having none will be offset by the larger family sizes of the younger, religiously affiliated population.[61] Kaufman, Goujon, and Skirbekk suggest that, all other things remaining equal, the religious decline that has long characterized northwestern Europe could reverse itself by 2050 owing to steady immigration from more religious countries and higher birth rates among the religious than the nonreligious.[62]

Much attention is given to religious trends—past, present, and future— in the United States and other countries, and changes are often theorized as individual-level changes in religious beliefs or practices and how they aggregate over time. However, these types of change are only part of what

Box 5 RELIGIOUS COMPOSITION OF COUNTRIES
AROUND THE WORLD

If you are interested in learning more about how the religious composition of different regions or countries worldwide is projected to
change, we recommend exploring the Pew Research Center's
Religion and Public Life report entitled, "Religious Composition by
Country, 2010–2050."[1]

There, you are able to view projections of religious composition
for regions or countries by decade. You can click on a religion to then
have the data table ordered by largest to smallest or vice versa. Look
up countries or regions that interest you and see if your projections
about change over time line up with what they have predicted.

1 Pew Research Center 2015b.

determines the religiousness of a nation. Other demographic patterns and
processes—such as fertility, migration, mortality, or the other compositional changes noted in this chapter—can result in fluctuations in religiousness at the population level even when no single individual switches
her affiliation or alters how often she attends or prays. The advantage of a
demographic perspective on the religious nature of a population and its
changes over time is being able to conceptualize, explain, and predict how
all these processes simultaneously shape the religious fabric of a society.

4 Change in America's Congregations

Much of religious life in the United States takes place within institutions designated for piety and worship such as churches, synagogues, temples, and mosques. A general term encompassing these types of religious institutions is a "congregation."[1] Congregations exist for almost all religious traditions in the United States. Even religions that do not usually involve weekly worship gatherings (e.g., Hinduism) often make use of this form in the United States in a process called de facto congregationalism.[2]

It is essential in a book about understanding complexities in the religious landscape of the United States to supplement trends in how Americans characterize their own religious identity, beliefs, and practices with a view of how congregations have changed (or not) over time. Throughout this chapter we often refer to "religious congregations" in general. This is because the ideas we discuss and the national data we present involve institutions from a variety of religions. However, it is certainly the case that Christian congregations far outnumber other religious institutions in the United States, so the patterns we describe often represent Christian groups best. When a study or theory we cite is limited to Christian congregations, or even to a particular Christian group, we will acknowledge this by talking about churches or a particular denomination within Christianity.

It is difficult to estimate the number of religious congregations in the United States at any point in time because there are so many scattered across the country, and there is a constant flux of congregations forming and dissolving. The best estimates available come from the National Congregations Study (NCS), directed by Professor Mark Chaves at Duke University and conducted in 1998, 2006, and 2012.[3]

One helpful aspect of the NCS is that the data can be analyzed both in terms of congregations and of congregation attendees.[4] For example, we document below a trend in the average congregation size shrinking while the average person is attending a congregation that is increasingly larger. While this might initially sound counterintuitive, the two facts represent different aspects of trends in congregations in the United States. These two perspectives allow us to track trends in the numbers and makeup of congregations and in the changes attendees may notice in their own congregations. Because these vantage points are useful, we cover both of them in this chapter.

Data from the NCS suggest that although there was a slight increase in the number of congregations between 1998 and 2007, the total number of religious congregations in the United States has remained just over three hundred thousand for a couple of decades.[5] The relative stability in the number of religious congregations in the United States is likely the result of two factors: congregations have a very low rate of failure, with many continuing to operate even with only a few members; and the number of nondenominational churches has been increasing.[6] The number of congregations without an official denominational affiliation increased from 18 percent in 1998 to 24 percent in 2012.[7] Religious congregations have more members than any other voluntary organizations in the United States, which serves as another indicator of their importance in society.[8]

In keeping with our comment in chapter 2 on the limitations of using large, national surveys to study small racial and ethnic minority groups we should sound a similar note of caution here that the NCS results are less useful in understanding the characteristics and trends for less populous and non-Christian religious congregations. While de facto congregationalism is a general pattern that applies to many minority religious groups, important ethnographic and interview-based studies show considerable variation across religious organizations. For example, while affirming

Box 6 GEOGRAPHIC VARIATION

Interested in the location of all these congregations? The ARDA has interactive maps where you can plot the number of congregations across the United States.[1]

As an additional step, you can plot other measures of interest that vary geographically, including crime statistics, voting behaviors, and demographic variables. As you explore these maps, think through the following questions: How well does the number of congregations match with the other measures you investigate? What surprises you about the variation in these variables by state and region? Do you think there is a direct link between the number of congregations in an area and the other outcomes you plotted, or is there something else about that state or region that would explain the variation?

1 "U.S. Congregational Data: Maps," Association of Religion Database, accessed January 20, 2020, http://www.thearda.com/mapsReports/maps/Ardamap.asp?mo1 =2001&alpha=&GRP2=1&map2=1.

common characteristics across religious groups in the United States, a study of Thai Buddhist temples has called for attention to the ways organizations remain diverse and distinctive.[9] As a result, while many of the trends discussed in this chapter may be relevant to other religious groups, our review of the literature, on average, will be most reflective of Christian congregations in the United States.

In this chapter, we highlight two trends in congregations: the increasing concentration of people in larger congregations; and the growing diversity across and within congregations. Both trends are significant not only for understanding religious behavior in the United States but also for understanding the role of religious institutions in society more broadly. The growing concentration of people in larger congregations is accompanied by the increasing visibility of congregations and the increased power for the leaders of these congregations.[10] For example, Pastor Rick Warren of Saddleback Church, one of the prototypical megachurches, interviewed both John McCain and Barack Obama before the US Presidential Election of 2008.[11] Multiracial congregations, a small but growing category, have the significance of bridging racial divides in a society in which most of our interactions and institutions remain heavily segregated. In analyzing how religious institutions are changing over time, we are able to consider where religious involvement and organizations in the United States may be headed in the future.

MORE PEOPLE IN LARGER CONGREGATIONS

Trends, History, and Characteristics

Over the last half century, there has been a trend toward the increasing concentration of religiously involved people in the largest congregations. This trend is accompanied by one that seems contradictory: the average congregation size has been shrinking.[12] The median number of regular participants in a congregation decreased from eighty to seventy people between 1998 and 2012.[13] This means that 50 percent of religious congregations in the United States have fewer than seventy participants in any given week. However, if we look at congregation size over time from the perspective of an individual religious participant, the average churchgoer in 1998 participated in a congregation with a median of 275 regular attendees, while in 2012 this number had grown to 310. In other words, although most congregations are small, more people attend large congregations than small ones.[14] The increasing accumulation of people into large congregations over time further accentuates this paradox.

This growing concentration of religious adherents in larger congregations is a trend that has occurred across all Protestant denominations that have collected data over time, starting in the 1970s.[15] Data limitations prevent us from tracking whether a similar pattern has occurred for Catholics, but data reveal that this does not appear to be happening for synagogues.[16] Among Protestant congregations, however, this trend has yet to plateau or turn around.[17] Large congregations experience their own turnover, since the biggest church in a denomination typically holds that rank for only about twenty to thirty years before it is surpassed by another church.[18]

Megachurches are certainly a part of this trend, as we will see later in this chapter, but they are not its entirety. Rather, people are not simply flocking to megachurches but are moving into slightly larger congregations across faith groups.[19] This detail is key because the growth of large churches is not the result of these churches attracting large numbers of the previously unaffiliated or nonattendees. In other words, an increase in rates of religious service attendance has not accompanied the growth of large churches, so this concentrated growth trend is the result of people moving from small congregations to large ones and not of a sudden revival among the religiously uninvolved population.[20] These large congregations are often located on the edge of suburban areas and end up being close to other large congregations seeking cheap real estate and land.[21] They have also sparked a new social organization of religion—multisite churches or churches that expand by developing satellite churches in neighboring areas that often video broadcast the same sermon to all locations simultaneously. These multisite churches are now the religious homes of about 10 percent of churchgoers.[22]

Scholars have offered a few explanations for this trend of larger congregations, including the obvious benefits amassing congregants offers, such as greater potential for financial giving or the economies of scale that are possible (in other words, lower costs when there are higher numbers of attendees). Other explanations include the broader trends of suburbanization and decreasing travel costs.[23] One of the simplest explanations for growing concentration overall is that rising costs make it harder to be a small church. As a result, small churches may have to make sacrifices in their programming and staff, and attendees may choose to leave those churches in favor of large congregations that offer more ministries and activities.[24] While this theory has not been confirmed empirically, it fits logically with the dual trends of shrinking average congregation size and growing numbers of attendees in places where most people worship.

Because this trend toward increased concentration is still somewhat recent, researchers are just uncovering the implications of these congregations' existence and in what ways they may be different from other congregations. The size of a congregation matters because it shapes the level of resources, the number of staff, and the programming options needed, while also contributing to bureaucracy and complexity. This can all come at the cost of congregations feeling less intimate.[25] However, participation and involvement can also vary with congregation size. People in larger churches tend to both attend and donate less than those in smaller churches: this might be a causal relationship; or it might be that some other set of factors, such as age, predisposes certain individuals both to attend large congregations and to donate less money.[26] Those who attend larger congregations also report expecting less social support from people in their churches and a lower sense of belonging than those who attend smaller congregations.[27] Because of these negative side effects of larger congregations, some scholars speculate that growing attendance at these institutions may ultimately lead to declines in religious service attendance as more people join large churches but then leave them for the reasons listed above.[28]

Additionally, the ratio of staff to attendees tends to increase in large congregations. This balance could suggest either that the staff in large congregations are more efficient or that they take on fewer ministerial roles and do less.[29] However, these staff members also wield greater power both in the public and within denominations than in smaller congregations for two key reasons.[30] First, having greater numbers of followers means that these pastors and staff have a large audience. Second, it also means denominations that oversee these congregations may be more likely to serve their preferences or needs. If denominations support a program for a large congregation, then denominations are supporting more of their affiliates than if they were to prioritize a church with only one hundred weekly attendees.[31] In these ways, the concentration of people into larger churches has implications for both the social organization of religion as well as the future of religious participation at the individual level.

The Case of Megachurches

Megachurches, or religious congregations that have upward of two thousand attendees per week, represent the extreme end of the trend toward larger congregations.[32] They have garnered significant public and scholarly attention.

Megachurches are not a new organizational form. Rather, scholars can find examples of large churches that resemble the modern megachurch as far back as the sixteenth and seventeenth centuries.[33] In the past few decades, though, megachurches have experienced higher growth rates than other congregations, and they are geographically clustered in the quickly growing suburbs of the Sun Belt and Pacific coast states.[34] Most megachurches have predominately White congregations, but 12 percent of them have majority Black attendees.[35] There are also many predominantly Black megachurches in the United States that are similar in structure and format to White megachurches but blend distinctive aspects of Black prophetic theology.[36] Individuals who attend megachurches have higher incomes and education, on average, than those who attend other types of congregations.[37]

Although one-third of megachurches are nondenominational or not connected to an official religious or Protestant denomination, the two-thirds that have a denominational affiliation tend to minimize that association.[38] Whether affiliated with a denomination or not, megachurches are rather diverse in both theological orientation and style. Scholars have suggested four general types of Christian megachurches: Old Line or Program-Based; Seeker; Charismatic or Pastor-Focused; and New Wave or Re-Envisioned.[39]

While megachurches are certainly an important trend in the United States, this trend is not uniquely American. The number of megachurches globally has increased dramatically over the past fifty years.[40] The largest megachurch in the world, with an estimated 480,000 congregants, is Yoido Full Gospel Church, located in Seoul, Korea.[41]

Explanations for the rise of megachurches mirror those for the trend toward larger congregations in general. Scholars have credited worldwide population growth, increased migration and urbanization, and technological advancement as explanations for the expansion of megachurches.[42] Focusing on megachurches in the United States, many scholars argue these particular congregations suit the distinct preferences of middle-class baby boomers and younger generations, with their distance from denominational identity and their integration of secular entertainment and music styles.[43] Megachurches also grow because their members tend to have more children than the general population and because they are particularly dedicated to recruiting and retaining attendees.[44] Although megachurches face similar challenges to all larger congregations, such as less institutional engagement of the average attendee, they are often highly intentional about overcoming these obstacles and structure activities to create intimacy and belonging at a more local level.[45]

Megachurches have unique implications for religion in the United States. Since megachurches generally subscribe to an Evangelical Protestant style and theology, they are contributing to periods of growth and stability in the numbers of those in the United States who affiliate with Evangelical Protestantism. Being typically unaffiliated with official denominations also fuels the shift toward nondenominationalism in the United States.[46] Additionally, while social service activities are often part of the work of congregations, megachurches have their own distinct patterns.[47] Megachurches are typically located in affluent urban and suburban areas, so their ministries and social service programs are primarily concentrated within those areas. Thus, they mainly serve relatively privileged communities and they tend to be inconveniently located for members of disadvantaged communities.[48] Research shows that megachurch attendees are less likely than other religious adherents to participate in a service group, advocacy group, or to work with others to solve a community problem.[49] In these ways, the increasing involvement of religious individuals in megachurches may reduce the extent to which religious institutions and their members are involved in service work to assist less fortunate members of society.

The trend toward larger churches in general, and megachurches in particular, is an important dynamic in religion in the United States to monitor. Will this increasing concentration of religious Americans in larger congregations change how people worship or observe their religion or how religious institutions operate in society? Will people become increasingly less engaged in the activities of congregations? Will religious institutions, in turn, play less and less of a role in meeting the material and emotional needs of the population?

INCREASING DIVERSITY ACROSS AND WITHIN US CONGREGATIONS

Trends in Types of Congregations

A second key trend for religious congregations in the United States is increasing religious, racial, and ethnic diversity, including diversity across and within congregations. The population of congregations is growing more diverse largely owing to the slight increase in non-Christian congregations (e.g., Jewish, Muslim, or Hindu) that has accompanied migration.[50] While Muslims remain a very small religious minority in the United States, the number of mosques and Islamic religious centers almost doubled between 2000 and 2011.[51] Still, in 2012, only 6.7 percent of all religious congregations in the United States identified with a religion other than Christianity.[52] There has been increasing involvement in predominately Latinx congregations, with 7.7 percent of religious service attendees attending majority Latinx congregations in 2012 as compared to 1.4 percent in 1998.[53] This increasing diversity in the population of congregations is also partly the result of declining numbers of mainline Protestant congregations made up of predominantly White congregants over the past few decades.[54]

In addition to this diversity across congregations, there has also been an increase in the diversity of religious leaders. Pastors and pastoral staff were more ethnically diverse in 2012 than they were in 1998.[55] Interestingly, though, despite the upsurge of ethnic diversity, there has been no meaningful change in the proportions of female clergy members. While there has been an increase in the acceptance of female leadership, with 58 percent of congregations allowing women to be clergy, female clergy members remain a clear minority compared to males. Only about 11 percent of pastors of congregations are women, and those women are more likely to lead smaller congregations, have secondary ministerial positions, and serve part-time.[56] Barriers to pastoral leadership for women are even higher for women of color, and Black women make up an even smaller proportion of Black clergy.[57]

Trends in Diversity within Congregations

Racial or ethnic diversity of the members of congregations has also increased to some degree in recent years, although the vast majority of religious institutions in the United States remain quite homogenous. The literature on diversity in churches usually defines diversity as having no single racial or ethnic group that makes up 80 percent or more of the congregation. Using that benchmark, the NCS tracked an increase from 15.7 percent of congregations being racially or ethnically diverse in 1998

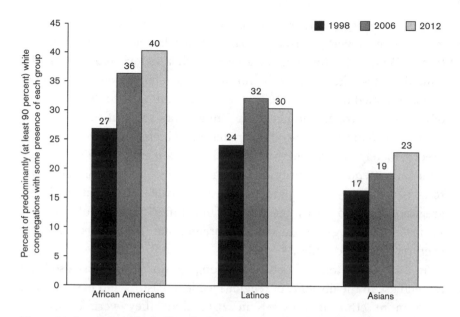

Figure 14. Increasing ethnic diversity in predominantly White congregations, United States (National Congregations Study). Republished with permission of Princeton University Press, from *American Religion: Contemporary Trends*, Mark Chaves, 2nd Edition (2017). Permission conveyed through Copyright Clearance Center, Inc.

to 19.7 percent in 2012.[58] Despite this increase, over 80 percent of religious institutions in the United States still have congregations that identify predominantly with one racial/ethnic group, usually White. On the other hand, the proportion of people attending churches that are entirely White declined from 20 percent in 1998 to 11 percent in 2012.[59] Likewise, the most significant trend in congregational diversity is that predominantly White congregations are significantly less White today than they were in 1998.[60]

Figure 14 illustrates the changing demographics of predominantly White congregations over time, showing the growth in those with a degree of African American, Latinx, and Asian members between 1998 and 2012. So, in 2012, 40 percent of congregations that were at least 90 percent White had at least some African American members (compared to 27 percent in 1998); 30 percent had some Latinx attendees (compared to 24 percent in 1998); and 23 percent had some Asian members (compared to

17 percent in 1998). We do not want to overstate the magnitude of this diversification because so many congregations remain at least 80 or 90 percent White. Furthermore, there has been no parallel diversification of predominantly African American congregations. They are at present no more likely to have White, Latinx, or Asian members than they did in 1998. Therefore, increasing interracial contact is occurring largely through minority group members joining predominantly White congregations. Whites, by contrast, have been no more likely to attend predominantly African American congregations since 1998.[61] Martin Luther King Jr.'s observation in 1960 that "eleven o'clock on Sunday is one of the most seg- regated hours. . .in Christian America" is still relevant.[62]

The small percentage of very racially or ethnically diverse religious con- gregations have received a significant amount of attention over the past two decades.[63] Scholars use a variety of terms—including multiracial, multiethnic, interracial, or simply diverse—to describe these congrega- tions. While they are referring to similar patterns, the terms vary slightly based on the author's theoretical perspectives.[64] For example, the use of "multiethnic" highlights congregations that bridge ethnic divisions, while the use of "interracial" draws attention to bridging Black and White racial lines.[65] Here, we mainly use the term "multiracial" but try to stay consis- tent with the researchers we cite.

Recent research has identified the characteristics common to multira- cial congregations. These congregations tend to be newly established.[66] One reason that these multiracial institutions tend to be organizationally younger is that it is harder to turn an existing congregation into a multi- racial one than it is to intentionally start one with the goal of bridging racial divisions.[67] In a study of congregations that were becoming more diverse, scholars found that attendance declined as a result of challenges associated with this transition.[68] Multiracial churches also tend to be larger than the average congregation, to have more young people, and to have more highly educated and economically advantaged attendees.[69] Racial diversity in the surrounding community is positively associated with diversity in a congregation, as well as with charismatic worship styles.[70] An important factor in both creating and sustaining a diverse worshipping community is having an equally diverse set of pastors and staff.[71]

As with other changes in religious life, there is considerable variation in the degree of multiraciality in churches depending on religious tradition. While the push toward multiracial congregations has generated reform-focused discourse and efforts in a variety of religious traditions, the success of these efforts has been limited. Most broadly, non-Christian churches tend to be most diverse with 28 percent of them qualifying as multiracial, while Protestant congregations are least diverse.[72] Within the Christian religious traditions, Catholic parishes are more diverse than Protestant congregations.[73] Shedding some light on these processes, Wright and colleagues found in a nationwide audit study that mainline Protestant churches reply to emails from prospective members with non-White sounding names less often than they reply to those with White-sounding names. Also, when they do reply, their messages to those with non-White sounding names are shorter and less welcoming. Welcoming differentials were not found, on average, in the email response from Evangelical Protestant or Catholic churches.[74] Though they are perceived to be more liberal and more egalitarian in terms of race issues, these results suggest that mainline Protestant churches, which tend to be predominantly White in membership, are less welcoming to minority group members than other Christian groups are.

In most religions or Christian denominations, as noted earlier, diversity tends to be the result of people of color, specifically African Americans, joining predominantly White worship spaces, rather than Whites entering spaces that are dominated by minority racial/ethnic groups.[75] As a result, Black Protestant churches tend to be less diverse than White Evangelical Protestant churches and have remained this way over time.[76]

Evangelical Protestant congregations were somewhat slower to take up integration as an explicit concern, focusing more generally on evangelizing friends, neighbors, or coworkers who, given the racial/ethnic homogeneity of people's social networks and neighborhoods, largely reflected the race/ethnicity of then current members.[77] However, their efforts shifted in the 1990s as they prioritized cross-racial friendships and communities in large Evangelical ministries such as Promise Keepers.[78]

Catholic parishes have historically been more diverse than other Christian religious groups because of their neighborhood-based parish model and their high proportions of immigrant congregants.[79] In many cases, this has consisted of multiple ethnic groups sharing the same space but by and large worshipping separately from each other rather than as an integrated service and community.[80] However, assisting immigrant communities in preserving their ethnic identities was one of the goals of Catholic parishes in neighborhoods with immigrant communities, so evaluating their efforts as successful or not through the lens of the typical Evangelical multiracial congregation is somewhat difficult.[81]

Explanations

Before discussing the reasons for the growing diversity within predominantly White congregations and the growing numbers of multiracial congregations, it is first worth considering the factors that push congregations toward homogeneity. The tendency toward homogeneity is not unique to religious organizations but happens across social organizations and networks as such. One of the main reasons is homophily, a sociological process more colloquially understood as "birds of a feather flock together." In other words, people prefer to be with those who are like them, which can include similarities in terms of race, class, gender, and ethnicity.[82] As a result, when it comes to voluntary social groups, people tend to choose groups with people who are like them: because people have many options for religious communities, the strong tendency toward homophily results in largely homogeneous congregations.[83]

One way homophily works in religious communities is that congregations attract new members via current members' social networks and from surrounding neighborhoods. Because members' social networks and neighborhoods are also likely to be homogeneous, this results in churches adding demographically similar members. Importantly, while dismantling barriers to racial/ethnic integration is important, homogeneity in congregations can have certain advantages. Religious organizations have a long legacy of serving as safe havens for oppressed and marginalized minority communities, including new immigrant groups and African Americans.[84] For some religious congregations, cultivating diversity is understandably a lower priority than preserving racial or ethnic identity and providing valuable reprieve from a world in which institutions devalue them.

Identifying what *causes* a church to become diverse rather than what factors are *a result of* higher diversity, or both, is challenging. Thus, many of the characteristics of multiracial churches mentioned so far, such as having a diverse pastoral staff and expressive worship styles, can simultaneously help congregations become diverse and be a response to growing diversity. Early research on how multiracial churches were formed suggested three primary impetuses for multiracial churches: mission; resource calculation; or external authority structure.[85] Some churches either implicitly or explicitly set out to be a multiracial congregation as part of their mission and to operate with a theological orientation toward bridging racial divisions or serving all people. Churches that seek to become multiracial in response to either declining or abundant resources, such as members or money, however, do so for reasons stemming from resource calculation. Lastly, in some cases the external authorities, such as denominational leaders, may commission certain congregations to focus on diversity to reflect their own goals for the denomination. Beyond these motives, churches may become diverse through a variety of methods that include reaching out to local residents when the neighborhood racial composition might facilitate diversity, focused evangelization, or merging with another church.[86] In sum, multiracial churches can emerge as the result of committed leaders—whether denominational or from the clergy or laity—who prioritize racial/ethnic diversity or simply a change in the local population affecting congregational demographics.[87]

There is ongoing debate as to how these communities are sustained once multiracial congregations develop. It is helpful to point out that while large national surveys of congregations are helpful in tracking broad changes in multiracial congregations, case studies of individual congregations have been important sources of evidence for understanding what the racial dynamics within these spaces look like. However, the variation in congregations means that studying only one or a few congregations at a time will not always provide the same explanation for why diversity does or does not flourish in a specific congregation.

For example, because racial and ethnic differences and indeed racism can produce tension, some scholars argue that "ethnic transcendence" is essential to the success of multiracial congregations.[88] In this case, participants create a shared religious identity that transcends their ethnic identities and becomes a more important bonding identity within a community. Others, however, push back against the idea that racial and ethnic divisions *can* be transcended, especially Black and White racial divisions. For these scholars, the power of race, particularly of Whiteness, remains salient in interracial congregations and organizations.[89] In one case study of a multiracial congregation, Edwards found that in order to remain interracial, the congregation would often first satisfy White attendees, creating places where White people are comfortable worshipping. This included making decisions such as minimizing discussions of racism during small group meetings and rarely having sermons that explicitly addressed structural racism. Otherwise, these communities feared that White attendees would leave, resulting in majority Black worship spaces.[90] How to maintain a multiracial and multiethnic congregation therefore remains an open question, and scholars continue to study the growth and survival or demise of these congregations.

Implications

While multiracial congregations remain a small fraction of all congregations, they are at least a growing one. Furthermore, they are a unique set of diverse institutions in the organizational landscape of the United States. Multiracial congregations are a *voluntary* social organization, and the separation of church and state means the government cannot regulate discriminatory practices. Thus, members of multiracial congregations are choosing to interact with people from different racial backgrounds. Scholars have long theorized that contact with people from other backgrounds can have positive effects on people's prejudices, so multiracial congregations represent an interesting site in which to study these processes.[91]

In some cases, participation in a multiracial congregation is associated with different attitudes toward race than participation in largely homogeneous religious organizations. One of the earliest studies on this topic found that White people who attended interracial churches had lower levels of racism than White people who attended predominantly White congregations.[92] More recently, another study has confirmed this idea, finding that Whites who worshiped in multiracial spaces had more non-White friends and reported higher levels of comfort with non-Whites.[93] Furthermore, participation in a multiracial congregation raises approval of interracial marriage and adoption.[94] One study compared two groups of Korean Americans: some of them attended a multiracial church and others attended a predominantly Korean church in a largely second-generation immigrant community. The study found that those in the multiracial church valued diversity and felt solidarity with other ethnic minorities more than those in the more homogenous congregation.[95] However, one of the ongoing challenges of this kind of research is assessing whether there is something about multiracial congregations that reduces racism, or whether those who opt into these spaces are distinctive and less racist in the first place.[96] Because other scholars have found no association between participating in a multiracial congregation and White people's views of racial inequality, the effects of multiracial congregations on racial attitudes are still unclear.[97]

Moreover, participation in these communities is not always associated with inclusive social attitudes and experiences; we see this especially when we consider how different groups within a congregation have varying experiences in multiracial congregations. For example, those belonging to a minority group in a congregation tend to have fewer relationships within the congregation, shorter membership durations, and more negative experiences within the congregation as compared to members of the dominant group.[98] There may also be an adverse effect of participating in multiracial spaces for people of color. One study found that African Americans who attended multiracial or predominantly White congregations were less likely to agree with structural views of inequality.[99] Again, this could also be the result of selection effects, meaning Black individuals who hold racial frames more like those of White individuals may choose multiracial worship spaces with White Americans more frequently than with other Black Americans.[100] Alternatively, this may also point to a bigger question of how multiracial congregations engage with issues of race, racism, and the underlying structural causes of racial inequality.[101]

Scholars have also examined whether racial and ethnic diversity in congregations is associated with other forms of diversity, such as social class or gender. For example, although some research has found that multiracial congregations were more likely to have socioeconomic diversity than more

Box 7 EXPLORING CONGREGATIONAL DATA

In this chapter, we relied heavily on data from the National Congregations Study (NCS), the only nationally representative survey of congregations. In highlighting these two themes, we have only scratched the surface of the questions you can ask about religion with congregations as the unit of analysis. Who are the people who lead congregations—how many of them are women, and how well are clergy paid? In what kinds of spaces do congregations gather, and what are their services or gathcrings like? In the ARDA module on Exploring Congregations in America, you can browse through the NCS data yourself to answer some of these questions.[1]

1 "Exploring Congregations in America," Association of Religion Data Archives, accessed January 20, 2020, http://www.thearda.com/learningcenter/modules/module8.asp.

homogenous congregations,[102] other studies argue that the ethnic diversity in congregations with high proportions of low-income people has declined.[103] Rather, wealthier congregations have experienced greater increases in racial diversity recently.[104] Additionally, multiracial congregations are less likely to allow female leaders, which is partly tied to their higher proportions among Evangelicals and Catholics.[105] However, conservative multiracial congregations are even less supportive of female leadership than other conservative churches, presenting an interesting puzzle.[106] Overcoming racism in congregations does not necessarily include overcoming gender and socioeconomic barriers within these communities.

Although most research on congregational diversity focuses on race or ethnicity, it is important to note that there has been and continues to be potential for increasing diversity in sexuality within congregations as well. According to the NCS, the percentage of churches in which gay and lesbian individuals are permitted membership grew from 37 percent in 1998 to 48 percent in 2012, creating the opportunity for increased religious involvement for these Americans.[107] There is still significant variation by religious tradition, with Catholic parishes showing decreasing support for gay and lesbian members between 1998 and 2012.[108] However, the increase in acceptance is likely not perfectly correlated with an increase in the (open) presence of gay and lesbian participants because there is an assumed conflict between most religious traditions and LGBTQ identities.[109] Additionally, a statement by a key informant that a given institution is accepting of LGBTQ individuals (on which this type of research is based) does not always reflect a completely welcoming environment.[110]

FINAL THOUGHTS

In this chapter, we highlight two of the key trends in religious life at the level of congregations: the increasing concentration of religious attendees into the largest churches, and the growing diversity (primarily racial and ethnic) across and within a significant proportion of US congregations. While there are other changing patterns for congregations, these two have particularly important implications for the future of religion at both the individual and organizational level. As more people become concentrated in the largest churches, these churches will continue to yield considerable power since their clergy have both a huge audience and a loud microphone. Although the growing numbers of multiracial and multiethnic congregations have significant potential for bolstering not only religious life in America but also race relations and stratification, scholars still have a long way to go in understanding both their advantages and their costs.

Understanding religion in American life requires this kind of attention to the diversity and dynamics of size and demographic composition because religious institutions play a somewhat central role in supporting the religious life of individuals. In other words, tracking trends in individual-level religiousness, like the previous chapters have done, presents just one perspective on the religiousness of the population. Knowing what is happening with religious institutions tells us about the state of religion in the United States, but it also reflects other societal dynamics, like the degree to which voluntary organizations are becoming more demographically diverse or not.

Of course, just because religion in America is currently organized in this way does not mean that the congregation structure is the only way religion can be organized. Congregations have evolved and adapted over time to fulfill the needs of particular groups in particular places. As mentioned in chapter 1, immigrant religious communities often provide particular services to meet the needs of newly arrived individuals. While not all congregations would offer help with finding jobs and housing or host worship services in non-English languages, these represent important aspects of some congregations.[111] Younger generations have also created distinctive organizational forms of religion such as "pub churches," online religious groups, and intentional living communities that give young adults space to ask tough questions about religion broadly and about religious institutions particularly but still cultivate social bonds and a sense of belonging.[112] In the same ways that religion has always been innovative at meeting the needs of new populations, the organization of religious life will continue to change and, in some cases, to resist change in a variety of ways.[113]

5 The Long Arm of Religion in America

Because religion and politics are two realms of social life that can be highly controversial, a familiar adage warns against talking about them at social gatherings. People hold strongly to their views of their respective religions and political parties as such. They can each be deep sources of belonging and provide roadmaps for how the world should work.[1] Religion and politics can also be combined into a powerful force, and, in recent decades, Americans have been increasingly aligning their religious and political affiliations, views, and behaviors in a bifurcated system of liberalism and conservatism.[2]

On the conservative side, increasing coordination between religious elites and Republican politicians and party leaders has often been attributed to shared opposition to abortion, same-sex marriage, other sex-related, personal morality issues, all of which are key aspects of the so-called culture wars.[3] Thus, it was perplexing to many that, in the 2016 US presidential election, many White evangelical Protestants and Catholics voted for Donald Trump, who had a very public history of sexual harassment accusations, infidelities, and divorce, not to mention an aggressive and bullying posture rather antithetical to the commonly held Christian virtue of loving thy neighbor. As early as the day after the elec-

White evangelicals voted overwhelmingly for
Donald Trump, exit polls show
By **Sarah Pulliam Bailey**

November 9, 2016 at 8:33 a.m. EST

INTERNATIONAL

Trump Elected President, Thanks to 4 in 5 White Evangelicals

Dramatic election ends with historic victory for Donald Trump.

KATE SHELLNUTT | NOVEMBER 09, 2016 1:39 AM

Eighty-One Percent of White Evangelicals Voted for Donald Trump. Why?

The role abortion played in this election might be bigger than many think.

By *Katherine Stewart*

NOVEMBER 17, 2016

Figure 15. Sample headlines following the 2016 election of Donald Trump.

tion, national periodicals displayed front page headlines underscoring the dominant role that religious cleavages had played in the election (see figure 15 for examples). The numerical strength of the White conservative Christian voting bloc in favor of Trump surprised many; however, tracing the development of how religion, politics, and race have been intertwined in the United States, as we do in this chapter, reveals a long history of well-coordinated cooperation between religious and political groups. To address this puzzle more fully, we will return to the case of the 2016 election at the end of this chapter.

On the liberal side of religion, social issues, and politics, two things are taking place. First, those whose identities include relatively loose religious affiliation or commitment to any religion and more liberal politics have been increasingly disaffiliating from organized religion. As demonstrated in figure 16, which comes from Hout and Fischer's analysis of the increasing rate of disaffiliation in the United States, it is the segment of the population identifying as politically liberal that has seen the highest rise in the percentage of people who have no religious affiliation.[4] Second, more theologically liberal religious groups, congregations, and individuals continue to mobilize politically as many before them had done (e.g., working

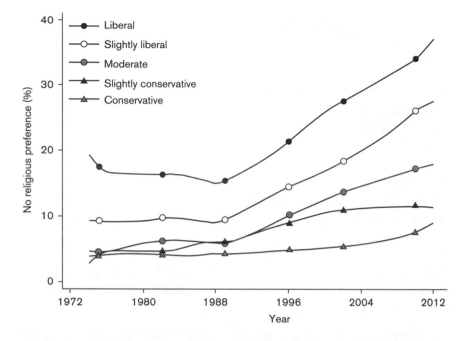

Figure 16. Proportion of population with no religious preference by year and political views, United States, 1974–2012 (General Social Survey). Republished with permission from the authors: Hout and Fischer (2014), "Explaining Why More Americans Have No Religious Preference: Political Backlash and Generational Succession, 1987–2012," *Sociological Science* 1: 423–47.

to eliminate child labor or sex trafficking). In fact, liberal religious political engagement groups, which were formalized in the early 1900s when the Methodists established an office in Washington, DC and were followed by similar advocacy efforts from other mainline Protestant denominations as well as certain Catholic and Jewish groups, were more prominent than conservative religious political advocacy groups up until the 1980s.[5] Contemporary forms of liberal religious political advocacy are active and are receiving increasing scholarly attention and media time.[6]

Throughout US history various religious groups have been motivated to adopt a range of causes, often taking different sides on an issue (e.g., the enslavement of millions of Africans) than others in their own faith traditions or in different religious groups. In all these cases, religious texts, values, and cultures have provided moral justification, and religious

Box 8 PERSONAL RELIGION AND POLITICS

In 2019, some media paid increased attention to the ways that Democratic politicians were embracing and emphasizing their religious affiliations and beliefs—mainly to counter the assumption that it is only Republican politicians who can benefit from sharing their religious convictions with constituents. For example, Senator Chris Coons (D-DE) has documented the importance of religious faith to his bipartisan efforts.[1] And 2020 Democratic presidential hopeful, Mayor Pete Buttigieg, spoke on multiple occasions about how his approach to faith and politics differs from others, saying at the second primary debate in July of 2019, "The Republican Party likes to cloak itself in the language of religion, but we should call out hypocrisy when we see it. And for a party that associates itself with Christianity to say that it is OK to suggest that God would smile on the division of families at the hands of federal agents, that God would condone putting children in cages, [that party] has lost all claim to ever use religious language again."[2]

It would make for an interesting research project to compare the social media profiles of a range of politicians from different parties and different regions of the country to assess patterns about if, when, and how religion is mentioned in posts. Burge (2019) analyzed the tweets of the Democratic presidential candidates in 2019 and found that Democratic candidates mention Islam more often than Christianity in their tweets.[3] What else can we learn from how politicians discuss religion publicly, whether in speeches or on social media?

1 Jenkins 2019.
2 Morris 2019.
3 Burge 2019.

institutions themselves have provided organizational, human, and economic resources.[7] In this chapter, we discuss how the relationship between religion and politics has been both a cause and an effect of demographic change in the United States. Our approach in this chapter differs from the other chapters in this book in that we do not rely as heavily on trends visible in survey data but instead describe a set of historical cases over time. In doing so, we suggest there is evidence for a common thread running through many social or political movements in which religion is involved: Religion and politics are often invested in drawing boundaries between social groups. These boundaries are driven by the desire to elevate and protect the cultural status or dominance of one group (often a religio-ethnic group, like White Protestants of one form or another) over others.[8]

Boundaries or distinctions made between social groups or individuals may be symbolic, conceptual, or social, and rooted in race, ethnicity, class, or gender.[9] However enacted, boundaries serve to separate individuals, building feelings of similarity and trust while also closing off access to resources and power.[10] Religious boundaries may separate the religious from the nonreligious,[11] set apart one religious tradition from others,[12] or may create new united coalitions out of individuals who would otherwise be divided by social boundaries.[13] Which religious groups are aligned with which political party or social movement has shifted over time, but the general processes are clear. When emotions are fueled—whether by patriotism or nostalgia (and the promise of a maintaining or returning to glory), by a deep belief in the equal worth and value of all humanity, or through the experience of marginalization and oppression (and the promise of emancipation)—religious and political identities merge and the institutions associated with these identities reinforce each other.

FROM THE BEGINNING: WHO BELONGS HERE

One way in which religion and politics have been intertwined from the beginning of White Anglo-Saxons' immigration to North America is in framing the questions of who belongs on US soil and who should dictate the terms of life here. Religious fervor has been built into American society since the earliest colonizers arrived from England following the zeal of the Protestant Reformation. These early Puritans were focused on purifying both church and society from the start, and they placed an emphasis on individual restraint and eliminating sin for the good of the community.[14] While many emphasize the religious pluralism that has been present in America for its entire history, it is important to keep in mind that White Anglo-Saxon Protestants were dominant throughout the eighteenth and early nineteenth centuries as a result of both their numerical majority and political preeminence.[15] They have also not often made secret what their motivations are. Jerry Falwell, a prominent Southern Baptist televangelist, founder of Liberty University, and key voice in the Religious Right once claimed: "The idea that religion and politics don't mix was invented by the Devil to keep Christians from running their own country."[16] While not the only focus of this chapter, much of our discussion will center on the boundary-making efforts of White Anglo-Saxon Protestants to maintain their power in society.

The Protestant Desire to Civilize

From the moment that the primarily White Anglo-Saxon Protestant colonists first arrived in America, they went to great length to "civilize" Native Americans and to coerce them into adopting northwestern European ways, including the ways of religion.[17] The colonists not only believed in the supremacy of their way of life and worldview but they feared that their own people's encounters with indigenous people would result in their regression to "savagery" and "barbarism."[18] In New England, Protestant missionary work was intense and resulted in a significant number of Native Americans converting to Christianity.[19] Following independence, the US government sometimes jointly worked with churches to Christianize and "civilize" Native Americans, often through education and often through more coercive means.[20]

Coercion and control were also central to the chattel slavery system in America during the eighteenth and nineteenth centuries. We reserve our discussion of that part of history for the next section, however, which focuses more squarely on racist boundary drawing.

Another group that powerful White Protestants sought to control, owing to a fear of their seemingly uncivilized ways, was the Latter-day Saints. Founded as a religious group in New York in 1830, the Latter-day Saints (LDS) faced significant persecution and discrimination in nineteenth-century America.[21] Quickly becoming a large-scale movement adhering to the sacred texts in the Book of Mormon, LDS faced immediate threats and rejection partly owing to their practice of polygamy.[22] Their leaders were driven west by violence, and Joseph Smith, the founder, was ultimately killed by a lynch mob. Brigham Young eventually led the community of LDS into what ultimately became the Utah Territory, but the United States Army invaded Utah between 1857 and 1858 because of opposition to Young's theocratic rule in the territory and polygamy.[23] Politicians, most of whom were Protestant, continued fighting to abolish polygamy with legal action, including a Supreme Court verdict in 1878 banning polygamy and the US Congress's disincorporation and seizure of the assets of the LDS Church.[24] Once LDS Church leaders changed their policy and officially denounced polygamy, Utah was accepted into the union.[25]

Perceived Threats from European Immigrants

As the religious ecology of the United States continually diversified and religious institutions grew in number and size, it was the rise of Catholicism and ethnic Protestantism, and to some extent Judaism, that became perceived as a threat to "native" Anglo-Saxon Protestants. Immigrants from southern and eastern Europe poured into the United States during the late 1800s and early 1900s. As the presence of new foreigners grew, so did xenophobia, or the fear, distrust, and prejudice toward those from foreign cultures.

One behavior White Anglo-Saxon Protestants negatively associated with southern and eastern European immigrants, many of whom were Catholic, was the regular consumption of alcohol. Therefore, many White Anglo-Saxon Protestant groups took up the cause of prohibition, of making it illegal to sell alcohol.[26] Their efforts culminated in the successful passage of the Eighteenth Amendment to the US Constitution, which made alcohol production and sales illegal nationwide.[27] In part, these efforts were geared toward limiting Catholic drinking.[28] US counties with higher proportions of Anglo-Saxon Protestants and those bordering counties with high populations of Irish, Italian, or German immigrants, many of whom were Catholic, were more likely to adopt dry laws.[29] The prohibition movement had a devastating effect on the alcohol industry, which was largely comprised of Catholic or ethnic-Protestant owned businesses.[30]

Although the prohibition amendment was repealed in 1933, to this day many US counties remain "dry" or have "blue laws" that prohibit the sale of alcohol on Sundays.[31] Today, the prohibition movement is largely understood as having been a movement meant to encourage abstinence from alcohol in a way that would result in a healthier, prosocial life. However, as we will document further below, what underlay many of the laws and social movements promoted by Anglo-Saxon Protestants was boundary-making in defense of their religio-ethnic identity.

Catholics and Anglo-Saxon Protestants also fought over the nature and content of public education. Though church and state were separated by the constitution, the power and majority status of White Protestants resulted in a public school system that used Protestant texts such as the King James Bible to promote Protestant values and to teach the Protestant religion.[32] Furthermore, antigarb laws were developed in the late 1800s to keep members of Catholic religious orders from teaching in public schools.[33] Catholics responded by developing their own private education system that, to the dismay of many Anglo-Saxon Protestants, received public funding in some states.[34]

Another way in which Anglo-Saxon Protestant groups exerted their historical privilege was through their support for birth control as a mechanism for limiting the fertility of southern and eastern European immigrants.[35] Although the United States restricted immigration from these regions of Europe in the early 1920s, millions had already arrived and settled in large, urban areas. Their presence sparked fears among Anglo-Saxon Protestant Americans of "race suicide" or the idea that they were being outnumbered by these immigrants, whose sheer presence and high fertility threatened them. The combination of fearing a loss of numerical dominance and being motivated by the idea that Christians had a duty to improve society (i.e., the social gospel) led to nine major Protestant groups being the leading mobilizers between 1929 and 1931 of support to overturn bans on birth control.[36] Wilde and Danielson describe this as a "racial project" founded on the desire to keep Anglo-Saxon Protestants in numeric and social positions of power.[37]

During World War II, an important example of exclusion of an immigrant group on the basis of race and religion was the case of Japanese internment. Japanese immigrants had experienced discrimination and exclusion since their arrival in the United States in the late nineteenth century.[38] The two main religions practiced by Japanese Americans during this time were Buddhism and Christianity, with both religions offering spiritual and social support, particularly to newly arriving immigrants.[39] Before World War II, Japanese American Buddhists had experienced marginalization for their religious beliefs, while Japanese American Protestants received some benefits for participating in the dominant religious group of the United States.[40]

Following the attack on Pearl Harbor, however, Japanese Americans were suddenly forced to leave their homes and possessions quickly and move into internment camps. Religious leaders played an important role in helping their members pack up, move, and store their belongings, with temples and churches functioning as storage centers during internment.[41] Within the camps, Christians had more access to their religious leaders, who provided support and comfort, while Buddhist leaders were more likely to be interned and prevented from seeing other Japanese American Buddhists.[42] However, formal religion for both Christians and Buddhists still persisted within the camps.[43] In one camp, there was also a resurgence of Japanese folk beliefs and practices during internment, as well as an emergence of study groups and clubs for traditional Japanese cultural activities such as drama, music, and poetry.[44]

As we will discuss further in this chapter, while race/ethnicity and religion can serve as a motivation to exclude those perceived to be a threat—in this case, Japanese Americans who were thought to be loyal to Japan rather than America during the war—it can also serve as a unifying force for those who are being marginalized and victimized. For example, religious beliefs and practices provided a basis for cultural resistance among Japanese Americans during their internment: core ethnic and religious beliefs such as loyalty to family (or to those in your camp) and ancestor worship promoted solidarity in the midst of oppression.[45] In these ways, Japanese internment represented both exclusion on the basis of race/ethnicity and religion, as well as the use of religion as a tool for resistance.

LATER WAVES OF IMMIGRATION

The role of religion and religious organizations in immigration policy and immigrant reception is complex. There is evidence that at certain times and for certain religious groups, especially those with an orthodox belief in their supremacy as a religio-ethnic group, religion is a motivation to exclude foreigners and slow immigration. On the other hand, at some points in history, certain religious groups elevate religious teachings about equality, tolerance, and service above particularistic tendencies, motivating a pro-immigration policy stance.

For example, due to the fear that immigrants with different religions and cultures would begin to outnumber and overrule those in power, many Anglo-Saxon Protestant politicians began making efforts to curb the tide of immigration in the early twentieth century. Quotas were established to limit which immigrants would be welcomed and how many would be accepted. These racist policies favored immigrants from northern and western Europe, limited the number of immigrants from southern and eastern Europe, and banned Asian and other immigrants entirely.[46] In the interest of recruiting low-wage labor, Mexico was later added to the acceptance list with no restrictions following World War I, but many Mexican immigrants were sent back to Mexico during the Great Depression.[47] By World War II, the United States had instituted a very restrictive immigration policy, setting quotas for countries that had previously been unrestricted and continuing the ban on Asian immigrants.[48]

However, following World War II, as a result of a combination of circumstances, like a booming economy and ethnic lobbying, these barriers began to be lifted; this included lifting the ban on Asian immigrants and eliminating the quota system.[49] There is some evidence that the National Council of Churches was one of many private organizations pushing the federal government toward immigration reform.[50] Moreover, when the Displaced Persons Act went into law in 1948, voluntary agencies such as the National Catholic Welfare Council, the Church World Service, the National Lutheran Council, and a Jewish group called the United Service for New Americans pledged to support and resettle more than two thirds of the refugees the United States was planning to accept.[51] In these cases, religious groups and individuals were present on both sides of the concerns over immigration.

Although immigration policy largely prohibited Buddhists, Hindus, Muslims, and others from moving to the United States before the middle of the twentieth Century, the Hart-Cellar Immigration Act of 1965 did

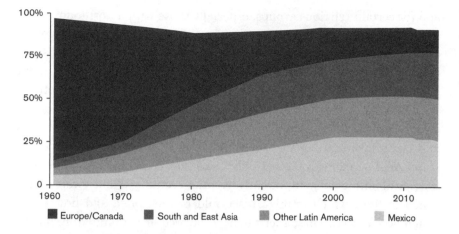

Figure 17. Origins of the US immigrant population, 1960–2015. This figure is reprinted from Pew Research Center on June 3, 2019, https://www.pewresearch .org/hispanic/chart/immigrant-statistical-portrait-origins-of-the-u-s-immigrant -population/.

away with country quotas based on prejudice toward non-European immigrants and changed the religious and ethnic makeup of immigrants in the United States.[52] For example, of the ten countries sending the most immigrants to the United States in 1960, seven were European and one of them was Canada; by 1990, however, six of the ten countries sending the most immigrants to the United States were Asian, and the country sending the greatest number was Mexico.[53] Figure 17 shows the resulting change over time in country of origin for immigrants living in the United States. European and Canadian immigrants dominated in the 1960s, but this was subsequently balanced out by growing proportions of immigrants from Asia and Latin America.[54]

In general, scholars have noticed that religious beliefs can predispose people to have both more negative views (and prejudice more broadly) toward immigration and more positive ones.[55] There is some evidence that religious commitment increased pro-immigration attitudes, at least around the time that the Immigration Act of 1965 was passed and in defense of Japanese immigrants.[56] Testing these ideas more recently, however, scholars have found that stronger religious identities are associated with higher support for immigrants who are similar to them in terms of religion and ethnicity, but that there is lower support for immigrants classified as others.[57] Fetzer has examined how religion was related to opposition to immigrants and support for Proposition 187, a California law that aimed to make undocumented immigrants ineligible for public services.[58] Because Jews and Catholics represent religious minorities in the predominantly Protestant United States, he predicted that these groups would be more supportive of immigrants with whom they share a marginalized status. In partial support of this theory, Catholics, Jews, and those affiliated with other non-Protestant religions were less opposed to immigration in general but were *more* likely to support Proposition 187, which limited services for the largely Latinx immigrant population of California.[59]

In recent decades, increased immigration from nations with large Muslim populations has presented a particular challenge for immigrant incorporation because many Americans perceive Islam as anti-Christian and un-American. This was exacerbated by the terrorist attacks of September 11, 2001.[60] As Casanova argues, the status of other, which produces distrust among Americans, is similar to what Catholics faced throughout the nineteenth and early twentieth century, as it hinges on ideas held about the compatibility of foreign religions (or ways of life) with what is often understood to be a Christian American society.[61] Recently, Islam has been subject to backlash from nativist Protestants; this has resulted from the globalized conflicts between Islam and the Christian West and the so-called clash of civilizations.[62] Americans report the least favorable views toward Muslims as compared to other religious groups in the United States, and rate them as the least "evolved."[63] Anti-Muslim fringe organizations have entered mainstream political discourse,[64] and Evangelical Christian rhetoric against Muslims has drawn increasingly sharp boundaries between Muslims and Evangelicals since 9/11.[65] As Americans continue to link national membership with Protestant or Judeo-Christian identification, Muslims and other minority religious groups are marginalized and excluded.[66] This issue is particularly important today given that American Muslims have faced considerable scrutiny under President Trump, with his calls for a Muslim register and travel bans.[67]

Examining the views and actions of religious groups toward immigrant populations over time reveals an underlying current of the urge, especially on the part of White Protestants, to protect group supremacy. The desire to maintain prominence sometimes takes a more religious inflection, such as the morally cast movement of prohibition, sometimes a more xenophobic tone, as with the eugenics movement and support for birth control (focused on immigrant populations), and sometimes a more nationalist or patriotic tenor, as seen in today's very tight pairing of conservative Protestant groups and anti-immigrant movements.[68]

An important counterexample to the link between religion and anti-immigrant attitudes is the sanctuary movement that emerged in the 1980s in response to the growing number of refugees arriving from Central America. Made up of congregations, religious leaders, and other activists, the sanctuary movement sought to provide protection and shelter for immigrants who had been denied political asylum by the US government.[69] More recently (since 2007), the New Sanctuary Movement has continued these efforts to protect undocumented immigrants following additional legislation against immigrants throughout the past decade.[70] The engagement of congregations and religious groups in this movement has helped to raise awareness and legitimacy for their goals,[71] and religious groups have justified their involvement in this political cause by centering it in religious goals, symbols, and ideals.[72] Religious activists have provided substantial support for the movement and have helped to change attitudes toward undocumented immigrants within their communities.[73] However, the religious wing of the movement has also dampened the political aims of secular activists by preferring to depoliticize their efforts and avoid calls for policy reform.[74] While this has had the effect of limiting the political victories of the movements, sanctuary movements nonetheless serve as a key example of religious institutions mobilizing on behalf of progressive and pro-immigration causes.

RELIGION AND RACIAL HIERARCHIES

Until now, we have discussed how religion and politics have become intertwined in response to Anglo-Saxon Protestant fears over indigenous people and non-Anglo-Saxon Protestant immigrants. However, there is an additional history of boundary making against the many Africans involuntarily brought to the United States as slaves. In this case, we see most clearly how religion can be used to support opposing sides of the same sociopolitical issue, as religious individuals and congregations have been defenders of slavery, advocates of desegregation, and everything in between. Antislavery advocates were motivated by the conviction that slavery was a religious sin, while defenders of slavery developed their own biblical justification for it.[75] What both sides shared, though, was the tendency to view the issue of slavery as a spiritual struggle of good against evil, with believers on both sides fueled by a desire to eliminate evil and sin.[76] With that powerful motivator on both sides, the symbolic and social boundaries evident in clashes over slavery and civil rights were particularly salient.

Between the end of slavery and the civil rights movement, Jim Crow laws legalized segregation throughout the Southern United States, lasting from the late 1800s through the 1960s. Though White segregationists and Jim Crow defenders were a vocal countermovement to the civil rights movement, scholars have noted the relatively tepid support many Americans showed for these laws by the 1950s. Many White southerners maintained support for segregation, but as the civil rights movement grew, fewer White southerners were willing to make sacrifices in their own lives and their religious communities in order to defend racial segregation.[77] Scholars have shown that religious service attendance was negatively related to support for sit-in protests among White southerners, as those who attended more frequently were less likely to support this form of civil rights protest among African Americans.[78] However, there was a clear divide between the pulpit and the pew on these issues. In fact, representatives of both the Southern Baptists and the Southern Presbyterians voted in favor of desegregation at their respective conventions in the mid-1950s.[79] Around the same time, Billy Graham desegregated his audiences while simultaneously attempting to downplay the race and civil rights aspects of this decision.[80]

The civil rights movement thus set up a contrast between Black civil rights activists (often clergy), who gained their followers' confidence and who realized massive mobilization through religious language and organizational resources, and White southerners, who were unable to rally their congregations to firm support of either segregation or integration.[81] Civil rights activism was dominated by Black churches and clergy members, most notably Rev. Dr. Martin Luther King, Jr.[82] Moreover, these leaders were supported by many White mainline Protestant churches, clergy, and ecumenical organizations that became active in the civil rights movement and were important allies in the efforts to pass the Civil Rights Act of 1964.[83] Through a combination of inertia, or a lack of willingness among White southerners to publicly support or defend segregation, and the recognition of this by Black southerners who targeted these weak spots, the civil rights movement was able to triumph over the extreme segregationists.[84]

As part of this discussion, it is worth highlighting differences between predominantly White and majority Black churches in terms of their political engagement. It is because of racism and discrimination that Black churches were established in the first place, and they largely continue to operate separately from their predominantly White counterparts.[85] In response to White hegemony and the need to survive in a society that has historically devalued their very existence, African American congregations have developed their own styles of political involvement and activism that are distinctive from White churches in a few important ways. First, while our discussion of the engagement of White denominations and congregations has mainly focused on particular issues that religious individuals and communities have rallied behind at certain historical moments, especially when their cultural dominance is threatened, the engagement of African Americans has been more constant. Black clergy overwhelmingly indicate their belief that congregations should constantly engage in and speak about social issues.[86] Since the post-Civil War, Reconstruction era, Black clergy have served in key political and intermediary roles between marginalized Black communities and the larger White power structure, and they are often respected as authorities in both political and religious realms.[87] Moreover, while we have noted partisan elements in some of the political activism for White congregations, the political voice of Black clergy is often broader than support for a specific candidate or issue would indicate. For example, while there is considerable approval among Black clergy for more government support on issues such as poverty and healthcare, support is mixed for other partisan issues such as reproductive rights and capital punishment.[88] Particularly during the Civil Rights Movement, their engagement was in the interest of serving the individuals who were marching, not of a partisan campaign.[89]

Though the civil rights movement made tremendous gains for African Americans and for desegregation on the whole, battles over racial segregation within religious communities did not end there. Following the passage of the Civil Rights Act, public organizations classified as tax-exempt could no longer continue institutionalized segregation or racial exclusion. Bob Jones University (BJU), an Evangelical Christian university in South Carolina, became engaged in a battle against these provisions as it tried to defend its Whites-only admissions policy. Though this was clearly a racialized issue, Evangelical supporters maintained that they were fighting in defense of the freedom of their educational institutions; this was extended to mean in defense of Christianity. BJU ultimately lost the battle with the IRS and changed their admissions policy in 1975 to accept all students regardless of race. However, the university continued to speak publicly about its preference to not accept non-White students to prevent racial mixing.[90]

The racial integration of schools at all education levels concerned many conservative Christians. This motivated the proliferation of private religious schools throughout the United States. When the Brown v. Board of Education of Topeka decision in 1954 mandated the racial integration of public schools throughout the country, many communities, especially in the South, established White-flight schools or private segregationist academies. Some research suggests that these schools were formed under a religious guise designed to claim First Amendment protections and thus work around federal desegregation laws.[91] Resources to found and sustain these private schools sometimes came from religious institutions which worked to establish and support these schools, as well as secular institutions such as banks, which worked to finance them.[92] In fact, enrollment in private schools affiliated with the four largest conservative Christian educational organizations increased 118 percent between 1965 and 1975 in the United States.[93] Thus, conservative Protestant private schools largely grew out of the creation of an alternative to racially integrated schools, thereby greatly benefitting, ironically, from being able to learn from the Catholic experience in privatizing education (forced by Protestants discriminating against Catholics decades earlier) and the use of public funds as a resource.[94]

Although proponents and some researchers have framed the growth over time of conservative Protestant private schools as a response to concerns over secular content taught in public schools and the exclusion of religious content or practices such as prayer, a desire for White Evangelicals to keep their children from interracial mixing in and around the 1960s was at the heart of the development of many Christian private schools and, arguably, continues to be so.[95] When nostalgia is invoked, and a return to "the good old days" is promoted as a goal, the public narrative around school choice emphasizes the need to protect children from secularization and subpar schools. However, research increasingly shows that a White Christian nationalism rooted in White supremacy, orthodox Christian exclusivity, and American exceptionalism fuels the private Christian school movement as well as many of the so-called culture wars we will discuss below.[96]

IGNITING SEX AND GENDER MORALITY WARS

These days, when one thinks of the ways in which religion and politics are intertwined in the United States, what often comes to mind is the Religious Right and its emphasis on "family values," which involves issues of gender and sexual morality such as gender equality, nonmarital sexual behavior, abortion, same-sex marriage, and transgender rights.[97] Since at least the mid-1970s, leading Evangelical Protestant figures (some of whom have also run or been elected to public office), such as Jerry Falwell, Pat Buchanan, James Dobson, and Mike Huckabee, have amplified the volume on calls for Puritanesque sexual morality and a general view that America was founded as and should strive to be a Christian nation.

Although a variety of studies of social attitudes, using GSS data, have shown liberalization since the 1970s in attitudes toward gender equality, divorce, premarital sexual behavior, abortion, and same-sex marriage, Evangelical Protestants remain less favorable toward these social issues or behaviors than others. Evangelical Protestants have exhibited a slower softening of opposition to same-sex marriage than the rest of the population.[98] Furthermore, as demonstrated in figure 18, the correlation between the frequency of religious service attendance and certain tenets of social conservatism has increased over time.[99] Steeper increases in these correlations appear to occur just before or after presidential elections, when

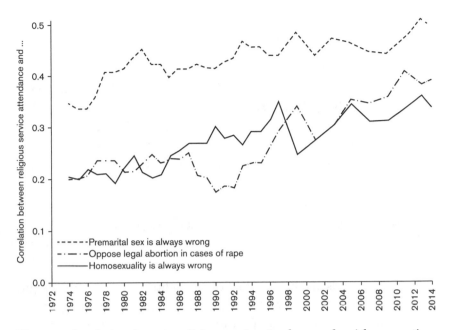

Figure 18. Correlations between religious service attendance and social conservatism, United States (General Social Survey). Republished with permission of Princeton University Press, from *American Religion: Contemporary Trends*, Mark Chaves, 2nd Edition (2017). Permission conveyed through Copyright Clearance Center, Inc.

greater public attention has been given to these issues. Also, since the early 1990s, religious service attendance has become more highly correlated with Republican party identification and conservative political views.[100]

There are a few possible explanations for these changes. One is that the American public is becoming increasingly polarized in their religious and political views. When the concept of culture wars was initially proposed by Hunter, it referred to polarization among religious elites over religious authority and morality. Since these issues of morality reflect their visions of what constitutes a good society, the passions and intensities of these debates take on a greater fervor than debates over other issues.[101] In the early 2000s, Protestant clergy were speaking from the pulpit in polarized ways on social issues, especially abortion, homosexuality, school prayer, and school choice. These issues reflect the concern over maintaining religious authority and morality. While there is some evidence for polarization

Box 9 RELIGION IN PUBLIC BLOG

For those interested in reading more about contemporary examples of the intersections of religion and politics, we highly recommend exploring the blog, *Religion in Public*.[1] Contributors share the latest data and findings related to religion's presence in the public square. Professors from different colleges and universities across the country have also posted their syllabi from religion and politics courses. This could be a great starting point if you are looking to do your own research on this topic.

1 *Religion in Public*, accessed January 20, 2020, https://religioninpublic.blog/.

in the data on levels of religious practice, but politics scholars largely argue that polarization and the "culture wars" rhetoric are often exaggerated. Indeed, national attitude data provide little evidence of polarization on social issues in the general public; however, US congressional representatives have increasingly voted on legislation in a partisan way.[102] In addition to discussing polarization, others have argued that there is an increasing "God gap," or a stronger divide between the highly religious, who are also more likely to be Evangelical, and the growing proportion of those who have no religious affiliation.[103]

Polls and social surveys spanning the last few decades indicate that Americans have remained rather stably distributed across the liberal-conservative spectrum on a variety of social attitudes.[104] However, there is some evidence that Americans have been increasingly changing their religious identities to fit their political views, so that may explain part of the increasing correlation between political and religious identities.[105] But there may be a more demographic or compositional explanation. The combination of decreasing numbers of liberal Protestants, which has been occurring since as early as 1850,[106] and declines in Catholic religious service participation, mean that increasingly the most religiously active Americans are Evangelical Protestants, a group more likely to be exposed to and agree with conservative social values.[107] Another reason for the growing alignment in religious and political identities in the United States might have to do with the work of political and religious activists on both ends of the spectrum who rally politicians and religious leaders to focus energy on mutually beneficial issues.[108]

While these "family values" issues receive a great deal of attention from political commentators for their close connection to religious conservatism in the United States, scholars are starting to question how well the link between the Religious Right and family values issues holds up to historical scrutiny. Roe v. Wade, the landmark case legalizing abortion in 1973, is widely considered to have been a catalyzing force for many leaders of the Religious Right in the 1970s. However, two years prior to this decision, the Southern Baptist Convention called for the legalization of abortion, and they affirmed Roe v. Wade in both 1974 and 1976 alongside other Evangelical leaders.[109] As governor of California, Ronald Reagan signed into law an exception to California's anti-abortion law for "therapeutic" cases,[110] and his 1980 campaign largely ignored abortion until as late as August before the election.[111] Jerry Falwell, already an Evangelical leader throughout the civil rights movement, did not preach his first sermon on abortion until 1978.[112] Similarly, it was not until 1980 when either political party declared a firm stance on abortion, and voters followed suit, adjusting their views on abortion to match the stances of their religious and political affiliations.[113]

As a result of this mixed evidence for the Religious Right's foundation in family values (even by their own accounts),[114] scholars are starting to call for greater attention to the racist roots of the Christian Right. A scholarly journal, *Religion and American Culture,* convened a forum of top religious scholars to write short reflection articles on how to study religion in the era of Trump. One common theme of the contributions to this forum was the need to recognize the role of racism in Evangelicalism, both historically and today. Racism is part of the boundary-drawing work we mentioned at the beginning of this chapter, as privileged groups attempt to close off their advantages and protect their status from the threat of outsiders (ranging from immigrants to foreigners to other non-White groups).[115] Rather than abortion or same-sex marriage having been the mobilizing causes of the Religious Right, issues such as school segregation and the Bob Jones case described earlier are what sparked this coalition and inspired their activism throughout the next few decades.[116]

To return to our opening of this chapter with the puzzle of why self-identified "family values" voters voted for a clearly antithetical candidate, it is vital to recognize the tight link between ethno-religious boundary making that is rooted in biblical themes with White Christian nationalist ideologies and xenophobia. Though Trump was not the first choice for many Evangelical voters, the proposals and condemnations made by Trump map onto the tenets of White Christian nationalism well, tenets that are increasingly common among subsets of White Evangelicals.[117] And, perhaps more importantly, the policy platform, as well as the stated and embodied values of Trump's female opponent, Hillary Clinton, caused far more fear and distrust (core emotions of xenophobia) than negative feelings in response to Trump's personal moral failings. For these Evangelicals, voting for Trump represented voting in defense of the (White) Christian heritage of the United States and the accompanying power and privileges that belong to these believers.[118] As documented above, this desire of White Christians to defend their status and their vision of the United States from the attacks of "outsiders," broadly conceived, is certainly not new, and it simply represents a recent example of boundary-making efforts of religious and political coalitions.

DRAWING AND DEFENDING BOUNDARIES

A thread runs throughout our discussion of the main ways in which politics and religion have intersected in the United States over time. That thread is a general boundary-making process in which religion is often invoked to define the good and bad side of a boundary. We focus on the US case, though these patterns are certainly not limited to the United States only. Across the world and in multiple religious traditions, including Islam, Judaism, Christianity, Hinduism, Sikhism, and Buddhism, religious ideologies and communities have both served and conflicted with secular political ideologies, groups, and institutions.[119] When religion is thought to provide a basis for nationalism, the conflicts can become particularly intense. Religious and secular nationalism provide frameworks of order and disorder on a national or sometimes even global scale, and their clashes can be magnified into sacred battles between good and evil.[120] Globally, these conflicts are also more likely to happen in places where the nation-state is only loosely defined, such as in Palestine, Sri Lanka, Iraq, and Somalia, and in countries where the surrounding nations have different religions, such as in Ireland, Poland, and Greece.[121] Within countries, religion can be tied to social and political movements, such as the overthrow of the Shah in Iran by Islamic activists in 1979.[122]

While these broad patterns of religion as a mobilizing resource and a boundary-making agent are evident around the world, the particular relationship between religion and politics within a country certainly varies by context.[123] While we have documented political polarization along religious lines in the United States, scholars of Israel, Turkey, Tunisia, and the United Kingdom, to name a few, have found minimal polarization in those regions by religion.[124] As Smith and Woodhead argue, religious affiliation was a weaker predictor of support for the United Kingdom leaving the European Union (i.e., Brexit) because there was not an alliance between a political party and a religious group of the sort that we see between Evangelicals and the GOP in the United States.[125] In other cases, religion may function as more of an indirect predictor of political support or beliefs. In a study of anti-immigration attitudes in multiple countries, Storm found that religiousness mattered largely as a proxy for identifying with the dominant social norms of a country and intending to defend those norms against cultural outsiders.[126] Since religion and politics both have their own individual complexities, how they interact and intersect in each country will be highly varied.[127]

Because religion and politics are social institutions that can be used to draw boundaries between in-groups and out-groups, they can easily cooperate to reinforce boundaries. Tranby and Zulkowski argue that religion can be a cultural tool used to draw boundaries around ideal and stigmatized gender norms, family forms, and sexual identities.[128] The same could be argued for political attitudes and behaviors. And political discourse is also a tool used to draw symbolic boundaries around acceptable religious identities and practices as well. Both religion and politics give us cultural narratives and symbols for understanding and interacting with the social world. It turns out that the coordination between religious and political cultural power is often motivated by drawing racial or ethnic boundaries and asserting supremacy and privilege. Therefore, we should be careful to not accept the surface-level explanations for the alignment of religious and political movements (e.g., abortion or other "family values") as the whole or even the main story, but instead look beneath the surface to the historical context and the common interests constituencies share in drawing in-group/out-group boundaries and preserving power. Religion has been a core factor in the structuring and restructuring of power and privilege in the United States.

Conclusion

AMERICA'S RELIGIOUS CONTOURS

Religion is central to understanding why the United States of America was founded and what makes it different from other wealthy, Western nations. Religious institutions and the religious beliefs and practices of individuals play a very influential role in daily life in the United States, and they have throughout the country's history. The religious composition and the levels of religious involvement in the counties in which Americans live shape their individual-level attitudes (e.g., tolerance or trust of others) and behaviors (e.g., divorce), regardless of what their own religious preferences are.[1] The more unity and interaction a religious congregation exhibits, the more its members report feeling a sense of belonging.[2] Education, income, and wealth are all associated with a person's religious affiliation.[3] Americans who frequently attend religious services live longer than those who do not.[4] Religion plays a meaningful role in a variety of community and individual processes and outcomes, thus making it imperative that we track, analyze, and understand the dynamics of religion in the United States.[5]

Any attempt to understand religion's place in American society over the past few decades, a time of great social and economic change, must involve more than simply considering the overarching trends of the entire population. In this book, we have moved beyond presenting aggregate trends to revealing interesting variations in religiousness across different social groups, and we have shown how changes in the relative size of these subgroups, as well as in age, period, and cohort processes, underlie the aggregate trends. Just as religion is likely shaping demographic processes such as birth rates, death rates, and migration, demographic processes are shaping religion in the United States.

Moreover, we have outlined changes in religion in the United States at the level of religious congregations to consider how the institutions religious individuals are attending have also changed over time. As religious congregations become larger and more diverse, the composition of religious organizations changes; this can have consequences for which individuals participate and how they participate. Lastly, we concluded with a chapter on the role of religion in boundary-making processes in the United States that have determined who is welcome and who is not. Taking a historical perspective allows us to consider how religion has consequences beyond individual lives in America, shaping how societies construct boundaries and national identities.

DEMOGRAPHIC ENGINES OF CHANGE

A demographic approach can complement other more common perspectives such as expecting country-level religious change to stem from individual-level rates of leaving or joining religious institutions or from personal decisions to change one's beliefs or practices. The discussions we see in the media about the past, present, and future of religious life in America often describe declines in religion as a result of younger generations and individuals or even large segments of the general population deciding they do not want to be involved in religion any longer. However, the trends we outline here show that independent of any single individual making a conscious choice to change, the population-level trends that characterize the United States right now, as well as universal demographic processes like cohort replacement, will affect the religious landscape too.

We have highlighted variance in the experience and practice of religion by demographic subgroups (e.g., race, gender, education, and their intersections). We show a slightly widening racial gap in religious service attendance and prayer.[6] The subtle decreases in both attendance and prayer noted by many scholars for the entire US population seem to be largely driven by what is happening among the White population. When it comes to gender, the growth in the proportion of the population with no religious affiliation is larger for men than for women,[7] although women seem to be narrowing the attendance gap with a slight convergence over time to the lower rate of attendance for men.[8] And, in terms of education levels, those with a high school degree or less seem to have had more of a decrease over time in their rates of attendance than those with at least some college. This is in line with other research showing that individuals who go to college experience less religious change than those who do not, though this may be counterintuitive to those who imagine that college is a secularizing experience.[9]

Although it is useful to parse general trends by one demographic at a time, we also know that identities or positions in various social structures (such as race, class, or gender) are intersectional, or that they interact with each other to result in different experiences for members of one subgroup who might not share another aspect of identity. Sociologists of religion have learned a great deal about how religion is lived at these intersections of identity through a perspective called "lived religion," or how people live out their religious beliefs and practices in material, physical, and commonplace ways.[10] Rather than focusing on idealized institutional forms of religiousness, a lived religion perspective works from the ground up, often revealing how forms of belief or practice are negotiated and adapted into one's identity. One substantial line of research taking this approach considers how women who belong to strictly patriarchal religious traditions come to understand their own selves and their autonomy.[11] Studies along these lines are usually ethnographic in nature, allowing for in-depth and intensive data collection and analyses to explicate meanings and processes that are difficult to represent or measure with survey methods. On the other hand, survey analyses and trend data are useful supplements to studies in the lived religion, doing religion, or even the newly-developing complex religion approaches. While never able to take as holistic and flexible a vantage point on individuals' lives as ethnographies can, the use of survey data to estimate trends at some intersections of identity allows us to consider how race, class, and gender differences interact with each other. It offers a limited but insightful approach that permits further investigation of the question, for whom is religion changing the most and in which directions.

Parsing general trends in religion by race, education level, and gender at the same time shows that the rise in having no religious affiliation is most pronounced among men, with White men (regardless of education level) leading the trend and Black men converging with them.[12] Among women, interestingly, White women have seen some confluence, with less educated women converging to more educated women's higher levels. Among Black women, however, there has been divergence over time, with more educated Black women remaining the most likely, by a growing margin, to have a religious affiliation. We see here the importance of simultaneously considering race, education, and gender in tracing trends.

Explicating trends in religious service attendance by race, education, and gender reveals more. Here we see that it is primarily lower-educated White men, and to some degree more highly educated White women, who have primarily driven the overall decrease in religious service attendance.[13] Another way to put this is that stable and high rates of religious service attendance among African Americans, especially African American women, have kept average levels of religious service attendance higher than they might otherwise have been. Others have pointed to increasing inequality as a factor in the deinstitutionalization of religious life among poorer Americans, and it does seem to be the case that lower-educated White men are pulling average rates of religious service attendance down in the United States.

Another interesting fact that emerges from separating trends by race, education, and gender simultaneously is that we see gender convergence in rates of religious service attendance for White women (regardless of education) and White men. For Black Americans, gender gaps in attendance have remained fairly stable. This is an area in need of more research. Scholars have theorized for years about the role of family and labor market variations over the last several decades in changing the gender gap in religiousness, but little empirical work to examine the gap over time has been done.

It is important to recognize that there are limitations and strengths of parsing trends by a couple of demographic groups at a time. First, we can by no means capture all of the meaningful differences within, let alone across, large demographics such as race/ethnicity, education level, or gender. Second, there are whole demographics missing here, like sexual orientation, (dis)ability, and place of residence. We are only scraping the surface in a way that pushes our thinking forward in regard to what the religious landscape of America is today, how it has been changing, and for whom.

On top of tracking subgroup differences, a demographic approach also considers how the population and its subgroups grow or shrink over time. One key trend that demographers are investigating involves the implications of the growing immigrant and non-White population. As the United States shifts toward becoming a majority-minority population in the next forty years, these newly arrived Americans will have significant effects on religious and other institutions.[14] Historically White religions and denominations (e.g., mainline Protestantism) are declining quickly as a proportion of the population. On the other hand, the Catholic population is stable.

There are other ways in which the US population has changed over time demographically, thereby playing a role in rates of religious affiliation and practice. It does seem that women's increasing education, labor force participation, and geographic mobility have dampened levels of affiliation and religious service attendance. For men, being less likely to have a pre-teen in the home and having more education may have boosted levels of having no affiliation.

Finally, mortality or death is an important driver of religious change in the United States. For one, life expectancy has been improving over time, keeping more elderly Americans around longer. Because older Americans tend to be more religious than younger Americans, when the elderly make up a greater proportion of the population, average rates of religious affiliation or practice are higher. Moreover, cohorts of people who were all born at about the same time tend to die at about the same time. Older generations disappear from trend calculations and new generations arrive on the scene. If each new generation is slightly less religious overall, the entire population slowly becomes less religious as a whole. There is evidence that suggests this is happening in the United States.[15]

As the US population shifts and changes over time, both as a whole and within its subcomponents, average levels of religiousness can rise or fall simply based on changes in the weight of any one group's level of religiousness relative to other groups'. This means that religion in America is not solely based on aggregating actual, individual-level change, such as giving up a church membership or deciding to stop attending religious services; rather, the country's religious landscape is also sensitive to ongoing demographic change.

These demographic trends are useful for better understanding the current trends in religion in the United States. However, they have implications beyond just individuals. We have mentioned the decline in religious involvement for less educated men; one challenge for congregations will be to decide whether or how to try to reappeal to the working classes that have left institutionalized forms of religious involvement. Some research has called for congregations to do more for those who are most in need of the instrumental support congregations can provide,[16] but this will require religious leaders and congregations to find ways to reach these populations. For some congregations, this may mean a reevaluation of their programs, worship preferences, and resources in order to consider what the barriers to Sunday morning participation might be for those who are otherwise regularly praying and identifying with a religious tradition. This link between how demographic patterns for individual religiousness affect institutional and organizational forms of religion is why our book also takes a congregational perspective on religious trends in the United States.

THE ROLE OF CONGREGATIONAL CHANGE

Having spent a great deal of time disaggregating general, individual-level trends in religion in America, we have also made sure to emphasize the importance of an institutional or congregational perspective on what is happening religiously in the United States. Our congregational approach focused on the dual trends of increasing concentration of members in larger congregations and increased racial and ethnic diversity within congregations.

Increasing concentration presents a significant challenge for smaller congregations. It will be harder to compete with increasingly larger congregations that can afford more staff and programs. In some low population areas, small congregations will be unavoidable; in other areas, however, there may be pressure to merge congregations or to grow in size. Increasing concentrations of more participants in fewer congregations also poses its own difficulties for those who manage large congregations. Some people feel that larger congregations are less intimate, and because attendees of larger congregations can blend into the crowd and maintain anonymity more easily, finding ways to attract and retain attendees will continue to be a challenge for leaders of these congregations.[17] Turnover and social distance in these congregations may ultimately loosen American's ties to organized religion.

When it comes to diversity of religious congregations in the United States, congregations of minority religions and congregations whose members are predominantly non-White have increased somewhat. Religious leaders or clergy in the United States have become a more diverse group too. Although the acceptance of women becoming clergy members has grown, the actual proportion of clergy members who are women has not.

The vast majority of religious congregations in the United States remain almost completely racially or ethnically homogenous; however, things are changing slowly. As far as the increasing racial and ethnic diversity within congregations is concerned, there can be steep barriers to creating and maintaining interracial congregations; it therefore remains to be seen whether there is a point at which remaining monoracial can be costly to congregations. As we noted, homogeneous congregations remain important to some communities, such as newly arrived immigrants and African Americans, so integrating all congregations is unlikely. However, other methods of bridging racial and congregational divisions, such as faith-based community organizing or congregational partnerships, could become increasingly valuable alternatives.[18]

We should also note that much of what we have captured regarding congregational change reflects traditional forms of religious communities. However, there is much to religion that happens outside of church-owned buildings and in ways that may not look like religion to everyone. The Emerging Church Movement (ECM) of the early 1990s brought about religious communities in new ways through web-based religious communities, "pub churches," and modern intentional living communities that resemble historical monasteries.[19] There have long been groups practicing mysticism and alternative forms of spirituality in the United States,[20] and the increased popularity of activities such as yoga and meditation suggest that people are seeking spiritual connection in old and new ways. When these forms of religion and spirituality happen within communities, they suggest that the social and organizational sides of religious involvement are still important. While the most common forms of religious practice may continue to remain stable or to decline, the ways new generations and groups choose to practice and live out their religious and spiritual beliefs, both individually and in communities, will always be far more varied than the survey questions used to track religion would indicate.

HISTORY REPEATS ITSELF

Taking a trip through American history, as we did in chapter 5, is a valuable reminder that religious and political coalitions are nothing new. In fact, the White Christian nationalism garnering so much attention in discussions of politics in the United States today has deep historical roots. However, as mentioned above, the increased presence of non-White populations in the United States and the trends in increased non-White and female representation in Congress suggest that there is plenty of room for new religio-political and religio-ethnic coalitions.

To demonstrate the long history of these tensions, we tracked how religious coalitions have fought to decide who belongs in America since the earliest waves of immigration to the country. Newly arriving groups of immigrants (as well as native populations who were here long before them) experienced the efforts of White Christians to civilize, convert, and restrict access to various social institutions and privileges. Throughout these efforts, religion and race worked to draw boundaries around particular groups to construct a religious, racial, and ethnic hierarchy. While this hierarchy has changed over time, White Christians, and particularly White Protestants, have sought to maintain their privileged position.

However, this narrative neglects the ways other religio-political and religio-ethnic groups have pushed back against this hierarchy and against oppressive structures. The civil rights movement is a clear case of a racial and religious alliance of African American Christians (with some White Christian support) advocating for equal rights. The continued political activism of many Black clergy members demonstrates the close link between religion and politics for Black Christians. Moreover, pro-immigration efforts by some Christians, such as the sanctuary church movement, represent another way religious communities and leaders have organized around equality and inclusion.

As debates between those with power that combine both religious and political rhetoric continue to rage over issues such as immigration and sexuality, they remind us of religion's larger role in structuring society. Religious change is more often considered at the individual level (or in aggregations thereof); however, thinking about changes in how religious ideologies and resources are used on a national level in defense of various causes helps us better understand unique forms of religious change and stability in America. While the alignment and cooperation between religious and political actors may not be new, the particular causes being defended and the religio-ethnic and religio-political coalitions being formed may represent new variations of a similar pattern. In our view, this pattern concerns who belongs and who holds power in society. This macro-level, historical view adds to the demographic and congregational perspectives we have presented to round out an understanding of how the religious landscape in America shifts over time.

WHAT DOES THE FUTURE HOLD?

Integrating all three of these perspectives—the demographic, the congregational, and the historical—enables us to consider how these levels of analysis interact. For example, we have discussed the growing racial and ethnic diversity in both the US population in general and in religious communities in particular. Thinking ahead, will the growth of racial and ethnic diversity continue to counteract the more substantial declines in religious service attendance among Whites? Will congregations continue to diversify, or does the discussion of boundary making in chapter 5 suggest that tensions in the United States over this growing diversity will contribute to a resegregation of religious institutions?

On the whole, levels of religious belief and practice have remained remarkably stable over the past four decades and have been resilient to dramatic social, economic, and political change. Despite marriage and childbearing having been increasingly postponed to later ages, the average number of children in families having decreased, and divorce having risen and then plateaued, families still strongly socialize their children to follow in their shoes religiously. Although increases in educational attainment and women's labor market involvement have taken place, similar numbers of Americans believe in and practice religion. In fact, a fruitful line of future research for religion scholars is likely to examine why certain societal changes have not resulted in more large-scale religious change for certain groups. Why, for example, has the dramatic increase in hours women spend working outside the home not lowered women's religious affiliation to the same level as men's? Why have more highly educated White women exhibited decreasing levels of affiliation and attendance, compared to those with lower levels of education, whereas more highly educated Black women have remained more likely to be religiously affiliated and attend religious services than less educated Black women?

Where there is notable change in certain subgroups, such as lower-educated White men showing the greatest decline in religious service attendance, will other groups follow suit, or will a change in economic opportunity reverse that subgroup trend and stabilize the overall level of attendance at religious services? Congregations play an important role in providing families with resources and support, but they also contribute to broader norms regarding what counts as a good family.[21] As family formation patterns continue to change and family types grow more diverse, the question of whether religious organizations accept or reject certain types of families—such as single parents, same-sex parents, or multigenerational households—will have consequences for which groups continue to participate in religious communities.

At the same time that there is a high degree of stability in America's religiousness, there is also no denying a rapid growth across all demographic groups in the percentage of those with no religious affiliation over the last decade. Researchers will be following this and investigating the degree to which these are inactive affiliates who feel freer to dispense with the religious label they were using before, or whether this really indicates a more general move away from engagement with religious institutions. Relatedly, it appears that some of the disaffiliation comes from those frustrated with the growing alliance between the Religious Right and conservative, Republican politicians and political movements. Thus, the shape that alliance takes going forward, as well as the ability of the religious Left to complicate the narrative about religion being associated with a conservative worldview, matter greatly for rates of religious affiliation in the future.

The case of the increase in nonaffiliation reflects the usefulness of jointly considering the demographic, congregational, and historical processes underlying religious change. The demographic perspective pushes us to investigate how the trends in nonaffiliation may be driven by demographic processes, such as cohort replacement. The congregational perspective asks questions about whether some characteristic of organizations is driving disaffiliation, such as the increasing anonymity in large congregations, or whether we should look to a different form of congregation where new generations are gathering. Lastly, the historical and political perspective helps us consider how the alliances between particular religious and political groups, such as the increasingly public link between Evangelicals and political conservatives, are driving disaffiliation. In this case, it may be that all three perspectives contribute a partial answer to this question and help us get at a fuller picture of this issue.

In these ways, we can say that what we do know is that life is unpredictable, but religion still plays a significant role in the lives of individuals, institutions, and society in the United States. It is likely that "In God We Trust" will remain the national motto of the United States, although support for its use will rise and fall over time. Moreover, different groups will find and support opposite meanings of the statement as the population changes over time. This is the American way with religion, and demographic, congregational, and historical perspectives help us understand why.

Notes

INTRODUCTION

1. Latterell 2011.

2. From James Pollock and Salmon Portland Chase, "Report of the Director of the Mint," October 21, 1863, as printed in *The Bankers' Magazine and Statistical Register* (1849–94), January 1864, 13, 7, 557. Cited in Latterell 2011.

3. Latterell 2011.

4. Latterell 2011, 602.

5. Latterell 2011.

6. Butler, Wacker, and Balmer 2008.

7. To see the most recent results for spirituality or compare the use of other terms throughout time, see https://books.google.com/ngrams.

8. Hill and Pargament 2003.

9. Hill et al. 2000.

10. Smith, Marsden, and Hout 2015.

11. As we discuss a change in the number of people with a religious affiliation, it is important to clarify what it means to have no religious affiliation. Researchers measure affiliation rates in the general population through sample surveys, and the precise measure used in the GSS is found in the following questions: "What is your religious preference? Would that be Protestant, Catholic, Jewish, no religion or something else?" So, the religiously unaffiliated are those who selected the category of "no religion." People could identify like this for a variety

of reasons ranging from complete disregard for religion to full embrace of religious or spiritual beliefs and practices but not within the context of an official religion or denomination. In fact, the religiously unaffiliated are a fairly heterogenous group when it comes to other dimensions of religiousness, such as belief in God, religious service attendance, prayer, or the importance of religion.

12. The term mainline Protestant originated to describe a subset of American Protestant denominations that took, and still take, a more modern approach to theology and emphasize social justice movements more than other predominantly White Protestant groups identified as Evangelical or Fundamentalist (Hadaway and Marler 2006). The word "mainline" is said to have come from the fact that many residents of Philadelphia's affluent suburbs along the Pennsylvania Railroad's mainline belonged to these Protestant groups (Lindsay 2007).

13. Chaves 2017.

14. Chaves 2017; Sherkat 2014.

15. Having no religious affiliation is more often a temporary rather than a continuous state. Cross-sectional measures of religious affiliation do not capture how individuals' religious affiliations may change over time. Hout (2017a) finds that between 2006 and 2014, one in five Americans was in a liminal state, religiously speaking, and that the same people sometimes reported a particular affiliation and sometimes reported no religious affiliation when they were surveyed three times, two years apart. One in ten Americans consistently reported no religious affiliation when surveyed. This suggests that those who are either ambivalent about or are changing their religious affiliation comprise a group twice the size of those who firmly identify with no religion across time. Interestingly, the probability that someone who is liminal eventually becomes consistent in his or her report of no religious affiliation is growing over time. Thus, part of what is driving this increase in the religiously unaffiliated is the growing number of persons who used to be weakly connected to a religious affiliation but who then drop their affiliation permanently.

16. Hout 2016; Sherkat 2014.

17. Kosmin and Keysar 2009.

18. Twenge et al. 2016; Voas and Chaves 2016.

19. Twenge et al. 2016.

20. Wachholtz and Sambamoorthi 2011; Wachholtz and Sambamthoori 2013.

21. Norris and Inglehart 2011.

22. Chaves 2017; Greeley and Hout 1999.

23. Sherkat 2008.

24. Chaves 2017.

25. Chaves 2017.

26. Chaves 2017.

27. Berger, Davie, and Fokas 2008; Gorski and Altınordu 2008; Norris and Inglehart 2011; Voas and Chaves 2016.

28. Norris and Inglehart 2011.

29. Norris and Inglehart 2011.

30. Hout 2017a; Schnabel and Bock 2017. However, see Voas and Chaves 2018 for critiques of this research and evidence of more equal decline in religiousness across levels, primarily due to generational change.

31. Hadaway, Marler, and Chaves 1993.

32. Grant 2008.

33. Finke and Stark 2005.

34. For a thorough discussion of the past, present, and future of secularization theory, see Gorski, Philip S., and Ate Altınordu, "After Secularization?" *Annual Review of Sociology* 34 (2008): 55–85.

35. There is a more detailed discussion of age, period, and cohort effects in chapter 3.

36. Wilde 2018a; 2018b.

37. This effort of parceling out trends for different subgroups could continue indefinitely if we divided by other relevant variables such as region of the country, urban and rural residence, age, and so on. However, constructing groups along the lines of race, gender, and education allows us to focus on important subpopulations that share a great deal in common and still track broad trends over time.

38. Chaves 2004.

39. Finke 1990; Stark and Finke 2000; Warner 1993.

40. Stark and Finke 2000.

41. Chaves and Gorski 2001; Voas, Olson, and Crockett 2002.

42. Gorski 2017; Whitehead, Perry, and Baker 2018.

CHAPTER 1. RACIAL AND ETHNIC VARIATION IN RELIGION AND ITS TRENDS

1. Camarota and Zeigler 2018; Massey and Higgins 2011.

2. James 2001; Zuberi 2001.

3. Chatters et al. 2009; Gallup 1999.

4. Hunt and Hunt 2001; Taylor et al. 1996.

5. Wuthnow 2015.

6. Brown, Taylor, and Chatters 2015; Matthews, Bartkowski, and Chase 2016.

7. Yancey 2005.

8. Brown, Taylor, and Chatters 2015; Hunt and Hunt 2001; Matthews, Bartkowski, and Chase 2016.

9. Hunt and Hunt 2001.

10. Taylor et al. 1996.

11. Taylor et al. 1996.

12. Gray, Gautier, and Gaunt 2014; Winstead 2017.

13. Hunt 1998; Hunt and Hunt 1978.

14. Winstead 2017.

15. Cressler 2017; Ellison and Sherkat 1990; Feigelman, Gorman, and Varacalli 1991; Pratt 2010.

16. Lincoln and Mamiya 1990.

17. Lincoln and Mamiya 1990.

18. Chaves 2004.

19. Tsitsos 2003.

20. Cavendish 2002.

21. Edwards 2009; Nelson 2005.

22. US Census Bureau 2017.

23. Pew Research Center 2015.

24. Matthews, Bartkowski, and Chase 2016; Putnam and Campbell 2010.

25. Matthews, Bartkowski, and Chase 2016; Suro et al. 2007.

26. Matthews, Bartkowski, and Chase 2016; Pew Research Center 2014; Putnam and Campbell 2012.

27. Matthews, Bartkowski, and Chase 2016; Putnam and Campbell 2010.

28. Hout 2017b.

29. Brown, Taylor, and Chatters 2015; Matthews, Bartkowski, and Chase 2016.

30. US Census Bureau 2019.

31. Lien and Carnes 2004.

32. Lien and Carnes 2004.

33. Lien and Carnes 2004.

34. Yang 2002.

35. Yang 2002.

36. Yang 2002.

37. Yang 2002.

38. Hurh and Kim 1990.

39. Min 1992; Park and Vaughan 2018.

40. Park and Vaughan 2018.

41. Suh 2004.

42. Zhai and Stokes 2009.

43. Min and Kim 2005.

44. Min 2010.

45. Leamaster 2012; Lien and Carnes 2004; Matthews, Bartkowski, and Chase 2016; Yang 2002.

46. Asi and Beaulieu 2013.

47. Arab American Institute 2005.

48. Read 2003.

49. T. W. Smith 2007.

50. We are grateful to Jerry Park for making these and other helpful points in a review of this manuscript.

51. To calculate rates of religious service and prayer from the General Social Survey data, we follow Presser and Chaves 2007 in transforming reports about how often a person has attended religious services in the last year to the probability of attending in a given week and how often a person typically prays to the probability of praying in a given day. Specifically, we converted the categorical measures of frequency of religious service attendance into a continuous measure using the following calculations: several times a week =.99; every week =.99; nearly every week =.85 (44/52 weeks per year); two to three times a month =.58 (thirty weeks per year); about once a month =.23 (twelve weeks per year); several times a year =.05 (2.6 weeks per year); about once or twice a year =.02 (one week per year); less than once a year = .01 (.5 weeks per year); never = 0. For prayer, we used the following numbers: several times a day =.99; once a day =.99; several times a week =.71; once a week =.14; less than once a week =.06; never = 0.

52. Sherkat 2014.

53. Finke and Stark 2005; Massey and Higgins 2011.

54. Pew Research Center 2014.

55. Matthews, Bartkowski, and Chase 2016; Pew Research Center 2014.

56. Mulder, Marti, and Ramos 2017; Ramos, Martí, and Mulder 2018.

57. Kosmin, Keysar, and Lerer 1992.

58. Park and Reimer 2002.

59. Park and Reimer 2002.

60. Matthews, Bartkowski, and Chase 2016; Pew Research Center 2015.

61. Fowler et al. 2014.

62. Brown, Taylor, and Chatters 2015; Matthews, Bartkowski, and Chase 2016; Norris and Inglehart 2011.

63. Brown, Taylor, and Chatters 2015; Lincoln and Mamiya 1990; Matthews, Bartkowski, and Chase 2016.

64. Lincoln and Mamiya 1990.

65. Shelton and Emerson 2012.

66. Shelton and Emerson 2012.

67. Lincoln and Mamiya 1990.

68. Edwards 2009.

69. Barnes 2005; Pattillo-McCoy 1998.

70. Ellison and Sherkat 1995.

71. Warner 1993.

72. Ellison and Sherkat 1995.

73. Hunt and Hunt 1999.

74. Eppsteiner and Hagan 2016; Hagan 2008; Hagan and Ebaugh 2003.

75. T. L. Smith 1978, 1175.

76. Yang 2002.

77. Massey and Higgins 2011.

78. T. L. Smith 1978.

79. Mooney 2009; Zhang and Zhan 2009.

80. Massey and Higgins 2011.

81. Min 2010.

82. Cadge 2008; Bankston and Zhou 2000; Warner 1993; Yang and Ebaugh 2001.

83. Eppsteiner and Hagan 2016.

84. Putnam and Campbell 2010.

85. Bankston and Zhou 2000.

86. Mooney 2009; Warner 1993.

87. Bankston and Zhou 2000; Hirschman 2006; Mooney 2009.

88. Lien and Carnes 2004.

89. Lien and Carnes 2004.

90. Hurh and Kim 1990.

91. Hurh and Kim 1990.

92. Min and Kim 2005.

93. Hurh and Kim 1990.

94. Emerson, Korver-Glenn, and Douds 2015; Zuckerman 2002.

95. King 1960; Tripp 2014.

96. Ammerman 2006; McGuire 2008.

CHAPTER 2. COMPLEX RELIGION IN AMERICA

1. We use "complex religion" throughout this chapter following the use of the term in the literature by Melissa Wilde and colleagues–for example, Wilde and Tevington 2015.

2. Collett and Lizardo 2009; Sumerau, Cragun, and Mathers 2016b; Walter and Davie 1998.

3. Beyerlein 2004; Lee and Pearce 2019; Lehrer 1999; Schwadel 2016.

4. Neitz 2014, 521.

5. Davidson and Pyle 2011; Nelson 2008.

6. Davidson and Pyle 2011; Schwadel 2016.

7. Davidson and Pyle 2011.

8. Smith and Faris 2005; Davidson and Pyle 2011.

9. Smith and Faris 2005; Davidson and Pyle 2011.

10. Davidson and Pyle 2011.

11. Sherkat 2014.

12. Davidson and Pyle 2011; Schwadel 2016; Smith and Faris 2005.

13. Schwadel 2016.

14. Boddie, Massengill, and Shi 2002.

15. Schwadel 2016.

16. Schwadel 2016.

17. Schwadel 2016.

18. Davidson and Pyle 2011; Park and Reimer 2002.

19. Schwadel 2016.

20. Lindsay 2007.

21. Hout and Fischer 2002.

22. Schwadel 2014.

23. To calculate these rates, we follow Presser and Chaves 2007 in transforming the categorical measures of frequency of prayer and attendance in the GSS into probability rates. In this way, the number represents the probability of an individual attending religious services in a given week or the probability of an individual praying in a given day. Specifically, we converted the categorical measures of frequency of religious service attendance into a continuous measure using the following calculations: several times a week = .99; every week = .99; nearly every week =.85 (44/52 weeks per year); two to three times a month = .58 (30 weeks per year); about once a month =.23 (12 weeks per year); several times a year = .05 (2.6 weeks per year); about once or twice a year =.02 (1 week per year); less than once a year =.01 (.5 week per year); never = 0. For prayer, we used the following numbers: several times a day =.99; once a day =.99; several times a week =.71; once a week =.14; less than once a week =.06; never = 0.

24. Davidson and Pyle 2011; Wilde and Tevington 2015.

25. Schwadel 2016.

26. Bengtson, Harris, and Putney 2013.

27. Lee and Pearce 2019; Pyle and Davidson 2014.

28. Darnell and Sherkat 1997; Sherkat and Darnell 1999.

29. Darnell and Sherkat 1997.

30. Uecker and Pearce 2017.

31. Keister 2008.

32. Keister 2008.

33. Fitzgerald and Glass 2014; Keister 2003.

34. Lehrer 2004; Mosher, Williams, and Johnson 1992; Pearce and Thornton 2007; Uecker 2014; Uecker and Stokes 2008.

35. Uecker 2014.

36. Fitzgerald and Glass 2014; Keister 2003; Keister and Sherkat 2014.

37. Granovetter 1973; Lin 1999; Mouw 2003.

38. Lee and Pearce 2019; Smith and Faris 2005.

39. Nelson 2008.

40. Edgell 2005; Sullivan 2011; Wilcox et al. 2012.

41. Mattis et al. 2004; Sullivan 2011.

42. Stark 2002.

43. Schnabel 2015.

44. Sullins 2006.

45. Kosmin et al. 2009.

46. Pew Research Center 2016.

47. Pew Research Center 2016.

48. Park and Reimer 2002.

49. Schwadel 2011a; Sullins 2006.

50. Schwadel 2011a.

51. Woodhead 2008.

52. Voas, McAndrew, and Storm 2013.

53. Avishai 2016; Collett and Lizardo 2009; Walter and Davie 1998.

54. Miller and Hoffmann 1995.

55. Collett and Lizardo 2009; Hoffmann 2009; Lizardo and Collett 2009; Miller and Hoffmann 1995; Sullins 2006.

56. Avishai 2008; Avishai, Jafar, and Rinaldo 2015.

57. Cornwall 2009.

58. Suziedelis and Potvin 1981.

59. De Vaus 1984.

60. Walter and Davie 1998.

61. Wilde 2018b.

62. Ellis 2018.

63. Ellis 2018.

64. Wilcox et al. 2012.

65. Lee and Pearce 2019; Pearce, Uecker, and Denton 2019.

66. Twenge et al. 2016; Voas and Chaves 2016.

67. Chaves 2017; Twenge et al. 2016.

68. Sumerau 2017; Sumerau, Cragun, and Mathers 2016a; Sumerau, Cragun, and Mathers 2016b.

CHAPTER 3. A DEMOGRAPHIC PERSPECTIVE ON RELIGIOUS CHANGE

1. Yang and Land 2016.

2. Putnam and Campbell 2010, 90.

3. Wuthnow 1998.

4. Wuthnow 1998.

5. Wuthnow 1998.

6. Putnam and Campbell 2010.

7. Wuthnow 1988.

8. Hout and Fischer 2014

9. Examples of more theologically and politically progressive groups include some mainline Protestant denominations or Rev. Dr. William Barber II and Liz

Theoharis's Poor People's Campaign: A National Call for a Moral Revival; Braunstein 2018; Delehanty 2018.

10. Yang and Land 2016.

11. Argue, Johnson, and White 1999; Hayward and Krause 2013; Hayward and Krause 2015; Schleifer and Chaves 2014; Stolzenberg, Blair-Loy, and Waite 1995.

12. Argue, Johnson, and White 1999; Ingersoll-Dayton, Krause, and Morgan 2002; Pearce and Denton 2011.

13. Hayward and Krause 2015.

14. Mahoney et al. 2001.

15. Wilcox, Chaves, and Franz 2004.

16. Mutchler, Burr, and Caro 2003.

17. George, Ellison, and Larson 2002.

18. Yang and Land 2016.

19. Elder 1974.

20. Hout and Fischer 2002; Hout and Fischer 2014; Putnam and Campbell 2010.

21. Wuthnow 2007.

22. Roof 1999.

23. Wuthnow 2007.

24. Schwadel 2015.

25. Bengtson 2013; Bengtson et al. 2018; Hout and Fischer 2014.

26. Chaves 2011; Voas and Chaves 2016.

27. Chaves 2011; Hout and Fischer 2014; Schwadel 2010; Schwadel 2011a; Schwadel 2011b; Voas and Chaves 2016.

28. Voas and Chaves 2016; Voas and Crockett 2005.

29. Greeley 2003; Schwadel 2011b.

30. Bengtson 2013; Hout and Fischer 2014.

31. Yang and Land 2016.

32. Schwadel 2010.

33. Schwadel 2011.

34. Voas and Chaves 2016.

35. Hayward and Krause 2015.

36. Schleifer and Chaves 2014.

37. Hout, Greeley, and Wilde 2001; Scheitle, Kane, and Van Hook 2011.

38. Dillon and Wink 2007.

39. "Religion in America: U.S. Religious Data, Demographics and Statistics," 2018, accessed January 22, 2020, https://www.pewforum.org/religious-landscape-study/.

40. Brown, Taylor, and Chatters 2015; Chatters et al. 2009; Taylor et al. 1996.

41. Massey and Higgins 2011.

42. Cooke 2011; Cooke 2013; Kaplan and Schulhofer-Wohl 2012.

43. Cooke 2011; Cooke 2013; Kaplan and Schulhofer-Wohl 2012.

44. Finke 1989; Rebhun 1995; Wuthnow and Christiano 1979.

45. Rebhun 1995.

46. Bibby 1997, 289; Bibby and Brinkerhoff 1994, 273.

47. Bibby 1997; Iannaccone and Makowsky 2007.

48. Uecker, Regnerus, and Vaaler 2007.

49. Finke 1989; Wuthnow and Christiano 1979.

50. US Census Bureau 2017.

51. Schwadel 2014.

52. Hipple 2016.

53. Hipple 2016.

54. Schnabel 2016b.

55. These figures come from multinomial logistic regression results for each measure of religion: religious service attendance; frequency of prayer; and affiliation. For prayer and attendance, we used the attendance and prayer rates we calculated for chapter 1 following Presser and Chaves 2007 and ran linear regression models. The continuous measure of attendance and prayer rates can be interpreted as the probability of attending religious services in a given week or of praying in a given day. For affiliation, we ran weighted multinomial logistic regression models. For each dependent variable, we ran separate models for each of our seven demographic variables (proportion with preteens in the household; proportion over seventy years old; racial/ethnic variation; proportion of foreign born; educational attainment; labor force participation; and proportion who live in a different city or state as compared to age sixteen). We also ran all models separately by gender. Then, with each set of logistic regression results, we calculated predicted probabilities for each category of the dependent variable by year (first year of data and last year of data) and each category of the independent variable. With these results, we calculated the expected change in each variable holding constant the change in each independent variable across the survey period. Then we added or subtracted that expected change from the actual levels in the first survey year to plot what prayer levels (or attendance or affiliation levels) would have been had this variable not changed over time. For example, the bar for preteens in household reflects what we would expect the levels of prayer to be in 2018 had there not been a decrease in the proportion of households with a preteen.

56. General Social Survey interviews were only conducted in English until 2006; therefore, the foreign-born participants were likely a select and smaller group than they otherwise might have been before that point. This means we should interpret our findings regarding the association between the percentage of foreign born and levels of religious affiliation and other variables with caution.

57. Specifically, we converted the categorical measures of frequency of religious service attendance into a continuous measure using the following calculations: several times a week = .99; every week = .99; nearly every week = .85 (44/52

weeks per year); two to three times a month = .58 (thirty weeks per year); about once a month = .23 (twelve weeks per year); several times a year = .05 (2.6 weeks per year); about once or twice a year = .02 (one week per year); less than once a year = .01 (.5 week per year); never = 0. For prayer, we used the following numbers: several times a day = .99; once a day = .99; several times a week = .71; once a week = .14; less than once a week = .06; never = 0.

58. Massey and Higgins 2011.

59. Cadge and Ecklund 2007.

60. Skirbekk, Kaufmann, and Goujon 2010.

61. Hackett et al. 2015.

62. Kaufmann, Goujon, and Skirbekk 2012.

CHAPTER 4. CHANGE IN AMERICA'S CONGREGATIONS

1. Chaves 2004.

2. Cadge 2008; Chaves 2004; Warner 1993.

3. National Congregations Study, 2018, accessed January 22, 2020, http://www.soc.duke.edu/natcong/.

4. Chaves 2004; Chaves and Eagle 2015.

5. Brauer 2017; Chaves 2004.

6. Anderson et al. 2008; Brauer 2017.

7. Chaves and Anderson 2014.

8. Ammerman 2005; Chaves 2004.

9. Cadge 2008.

10. Chaves and Eagle 2015.

11. Hornick 2008.

12. Chaves and Anderson 2014; Chaves and Eagle 2015.

13. Chaves and Eagle 2015.

14. Chaves and Anderson 2014; Chaves and Eagle 2015.

15. Chaves 2006.

16. Chaves 2011.

17. Chaves and Eagle 2015.

18. Chaves 2011.

19. Chaves and Eagle 2015.

20. Chaves and Anderson 2014.

21. Chaves 2006.

22. Chaves and Eagle 2015.

23. Chaves 2006.

24. Chaves 2006.

25. Chaves and Eagle 2015.

26. Chaves and Eagle 2015; Eagle 2016.

27. Ellison et al. 2009; Stroope and Baker 2014.

28. Eagle 2016.

29. Chaves and Eagle 2015.

30. Chaves and Eagle 2015.

31. Chaves and Eagle 2015.

32. Scott Thumma of the Hartford Institute for Religion Research has been managing a list of all the megachurches in the United States since 1992. See Hartford Institute for Religion Research, accessed January 22, 2020, http://hirr .hartsem.edu/megachurch/database.html.

33. Chaves 2006; Eagle 2015; Loveland and Wheeler 2003.

34. Ellingson 2009; Ellingson 2010; Thumma and Travis 2007.

35. Thumma and Travis 2007.

36. Barnes 2010.

37. Eagle 2012.

38. Ellingson 2009; Ellingson 2010.

39. Thumma and Travis 2007, 31.

40. Thumma and Bird 2015.

41. Thumma and Bird 2015. The size is reported here by Leadership Network. "The World's Largest Churches," accessed January 22, 2020, http://leadnet.org /world.

42. Thumma and Bird 2015.

43. Ellingson 2009; Ellingson 2010.

44. Ellingson 2009; Ellingson 2010.

45. Thumma and Travis 2007.

46. Ellingson 2009; Ellingson 2010.

47. Chaves 2004; Chaves and Tsitsos 2001.

48. Karnes et al. 2007.

49. Polson 2016.

50. Chaves and Anderson 2014; Chaves and Eagle 2015.

51. Bagby 2012; Fowler et al. 2014.

52. Chaves and Eagle 2015.

53. Chaves and Anderson 2014.

54. Chaves and Eagle 2015; Iannaccone 1994; Roof and McKinney 1987.

55. Chaves and Eagle 2015.

56. Chaves and Eagle 2015.

57. Barnes 2006; Lincoln and Mamiya 1990.

58. Chaves and Anderson 2014.

59. Chaves and Eagle 2015.

60. Chaves 2011.

61. Chaves 2017.

62. King 1960; Tripp 2014.

63. Emerson 2008.

64. Emerson 2008.

65. Marti 2005; Edwards 2008.

66. Chaves and Eagle 2015.

67. Dougherty, Martinez, and Marti 2016.

68. Dougherty, Martinez, and Marti 2016.

69. Chaves and Eagle 2015; Dougherty and Huyser 2008; Edwards, Christerson, and Emerson 2013.

70. Dougherty and Huyser 2008; Edwards, Christerson, and Emerson 2013.

71. Dougherty and Huyser 2008; Edwards, Christerson, and Emerson 2013.

72. Edwards, Christerson, and Emerson 2013.

73. Edwards, Christerson, and Emerson 2013.

74. Wright et al. 2015.

75. Chaves 2011.

76. Chaves and Eagle 2015; Dougherty and Huyser 2008.

77. Garces-Foley 2008.

78. Garces-Foley 2008; Emerson and Smith 2001.

79. Chaves and Eagle 2015.

80. Garces-Foley 2008.

81. Garces-Foley 2008.

82. McPherson, Smith-Lovin, and Cook 2001.

83. Edwards, Christerson, and Emerson 2013.

84. Edwards, Christerson, and Emerson 2013; Lincoln and Mamiya 1990.

85. Emerson and Kim 2003.

86. Yancey and Emerson 2003.

87. Yancey and Emerson 2003; Emerson and Kim 2003.

88. Marti 2005; Marti 2009; Marti 2008; Marti 2015.

89. Edwards 2008a; Edwards 2008b; Perry 2012.

90. Edwards 2008a.

91. See Yancey 1999 for an overview.

92. Yancey 1999.

93. Polson and Dougherty 2018.

94. Perry 2013.

95. Ecklund 2005.

96. Polson and Dougherty 2018; Yancey 1999.

97. Cobb, Perry, and Dougherty 2015.

98. Christerson and Emerson 2003; Martinez 2018; Scheitle and Dougherty 2010.

99. Cobb, Perry, and Dougherty 2015; Cobb, Üsküp, and Jefferson 2017.

100. Cobb, Perry, and Dougherty 2015.

101. Emerson and Smith 2001; Edwards, Christerson, and Emerson 2013; Okuwobi 2019.

102. Yancey and Kim 2008.

103. Chaves and Eagle 2015.

104. Chaves and Eagle 2015.

105. Yancey and Kim 2008.

106. Yancey and Kim 2008.

107. Chaves and Anderson 2014.

108. Chaves and Anderson 2014.

109. Sherkat 2002.

110. Whitehead 2017.

111. Eppsteiner and Hagan 2016.

112. Flory and Miller 2008; Marti and Ganiel 2014, 5.

113. Putnam and Campbell 2010.

CHAPTER 5. THE LONG ARM OF RELIGION
IN AMERICA

1. Edgell, Gerteis, and Hartmann 2006; Stewart, Edgell, and Delehanty 2018.

2. Brooks and Manza 1997; Hoffmann and Miller 1997; Manza and Brooks 1997; Putnam and Campbell 2010; Sherkat 2014.

3. Hunter 1991.

4. Hout and Fischer 2014.

5. Yukich and Braunstein 2014.

6. Braunstein 2017a; Braunstein 2018; Delehanty 2018; Wood and Fulton 2015; Yukich 2013a.

7. For examples see Smith 1996.

8. Edgell, Gerteis, and Hartmann 2006; Edgell 2012; Edgell, Hartmann, Stewart, and Gerteis 2016.

9. Lamont and Molnár 2002.

10. Lamont and Molnár 2002; Swarts 2011.

11. Edgell, Gerteis, and Hartmann 2006.

12. C. Smith and Emerson 1998.

13. Swarts 2011.

14. Fowler et al. 2014.

15. Noll 2009.

16. From a sermon given in Lynchburg, Virginia, on July 4, 1976, quoted in Goodman, Jr. and Price 1981, 91.

17. Thornton 2005.

18. Axtell 1981.

19. Axtell 1981.

20. Nagel 1997.

21. Fowler et al. 2014.

22. Thornton 2005.

23. Bushman 2007.

24. Bushman 2007.

25. Fowler et al. 2014.

26. Andrews and Seguin 2015; Gusfield 1986; Young 2002.

27. Gusfield 1986

28. Fowler et al. 2014.

29. Andrews and Seguin 2015.

30. Sherkat 2014.

31. Blue laws, dating back to the 1700s in the United States, are laws that forbid certain secular activities, such as drinking alcohol, shopping, or public entertainment. They are named for the blue paper on which Samuel A. Peters's *History of Connecticut* (1781) was printed, which listed activities to be avoided on Sundays. See "Blue Law," Encyclopedia Britannica Online, accessed September 13, 2018, https://www.britannica.com/topic/blue-law.

32. Fowler et al. 2014.

33. D'Antonio and Hoge 2006; Finke and Stark 2005.

34. Finke and Stark 2005; Fowler et al. 2014.

35. Wilde and Danielsen 2014; Wilde 2019.

36. Wilde 2019; Wilde and Danielsen 2014.

37. Wilde and Danielsen 2014, 1711. They build on the term used by Omi and Winant 1986.

38. Yoo 2002.

39. Yoo 2002.

40. Fugita and Fernandez 2002.

41. Yoo 2002.

42. Fugita and Fernandez 2002.

43. Okihiro 1984.

44. Okihiro 1984.

45. Okihiro 1984.

46. Reimers 1998.

47. Reimers 1998.

48. Reimers 1998.

49. Reimers 1998.

50. Kennedy 1966.

51. Daniels 2004.

52. Ebaugh 2003; Ebaugh and Chafetz 2000; Finke and Stark 2005; Sherkat 2014.

53. Jasso, Massey, and Rosenzweig 2003.

54. Pew Research Center 2019.

55. Allport 1979; Bloom, Arikan, and Courtemanche 2015.

56. Daniels 1977; Fetzer 2000.

57. Bloom, Arikan, and Courtemanche 2015.

58. Fetzer 2000.

59. Fetzer 2000.

60. Casanova 2007.

61. Casanova 2007.

62. Acevedo and Chaudhary 2015; Casanova 2007; Huntington 1993; Huntington 1996.

63. Lajevardi and Oskooii 2018; Putnam and Campbell 2010.

64. Bail 2014.

65. Cimino 2005.

66. Braunstein 2017b; Casanova 2007.

67. Lajevardi and Oskooii 2018.

68. Braunstein 2018; Putnam and Campbell 2010; Whitehead, Perry, and Baker 2018.

69. Stoltz Chinchilla, Hamilton, and Loucky 2009; Yukich 2013a.

70. Freeland 2010; Yukich 2013a; Yukich 2013b.

71. Stoltz Chinchilla, Hamilton, and Loucky 2009.

72. Park 1998.

73. Yukich 2013a.

74. Yukich 2013a.

75. Selby 2002.

76. Fowler et al. 2014.

77. Chappell 1994; Chappell 2004; Sokol 2006.

78. Andrews, Beyerlein, and Tucker Farnum 2016.

79. Chappell 2004.

80. Chappell 2004.

81. Chappell 2004.

82. Morris 1984; C. Smith 1996.

83. Findlay 1993; Fowler et al. 2014; Friedland 1998.

84. Chappell 1994; Chappell 2004.

85. Wald and Calhoun-Brown 2014.

86. Lincoln and Mamiya 1990; Sawyer 2001.

87. Day 2001; Lincoln and Mamiya 1990; Sawyer 2001.

88. McDaniel 2003.

89. Sawyer 2001.

90. Capps 1990.

91. Nevin and Bills 1976.

92. Andrews 2002.

93. Nordin and Turner 1980.

94. Sherkat 2014.

95. Balmer et al. 2017.

96. Balmer et al. 2017; Braunstein 2017a; Edgell 2017; Perry 2012; Stewart, Edgell, and Delehanty 2018; Whitehead, Perry, and Baker 2018; Whitehead, Schnabel, and Perry 2018.

97. Griffith 2017.

98. Hoffmann and Johnson 2005; Hoffmann and Miller 1997; Putnam and Campbell 2010; Schnabel 2016a; Sherkat 2014.

99. Chaves 2017.

100. Chaves 2017; Putnam and Campbell 2010.

101. Hunter 1991.

102. Fiorina 2016.

103. McCright and Dunlap 2008; Putnam and Campbell 2010.

104. Fiorina 2016.

105. Hout and Fischer 2014; Putnam and Campbell 2010.

106. Finke and Stark 2005.

107. Chaves 2017.

108. Chaves 2017; Hunter 1991; Roof 1999; Uecker and Lucke 2011.

109. Balmer et al. 2017.

110. Leavy and Charles 1967.

111. Balmer et al. 2017.

112. Balmer et al. 2017; Prothero 2016.

113. Putnam and Campbell 2010.

114. See Balmer 2007, 13–16 for an interesting description of how leaders of the Religious Right recognize that their success crystallized around frustration with the Supreme Court's ruling that Bob Jones University must integrate.

115. Lamont and Molnár 2002.

116. Balmer et al. 2017.

117. Balmer et al. 2017; Gorski 2017; Whitehead, Perry, and Baker 2018.

118. Gorski 2017; Whitehead, Perry, and Baker 2018.

119. Juergensmeyer 2017b.

120. Juergensmeyer 2017a, Juergensmeyer 2017b.

121. Barker 2009; Juergensmeyer 2017b.

122. Jelen and Wilcox 2002.

123. Jelen and Wilcox 2002; Zubaida 2000.

124. Gorman 2018; Smith and Woodhead 2018; Tepe 2013.

125. Smith and Woodhead 2018.

126. Storm 2018.

127. Jelen and Wilcox 2002.

128. Tranby and Zulkowski 2012.

CONCLUSION

1. Olson 2019.

2. Stroope 2011.

3. Keister 2003; Schwadel 2016; Smith and Faris 2005.

4. Hummer et al. 1999.

5. Smith et al. 2013.

6. See figures 2 and 3 in chapter 1.

7. See figure 7 in chapter 2.

8. See figure 8 in chapter 2.

9. Uecker, Regnerus, and Vaaler 2007.

10. McGuire 2008.

11. Avishai, Jafar, and Rinaldo 2015.

12. See figure 9 in chapter 2.

13. See table 10 in chapter 2.

14. Frey 2018.

15. Schwadel 2011; Voas and Chaves 2016.

16. Edgell 2005; Sullivan 2011.

17. Chaves and Eagle 2015.

18. Wood and Fulton 2015.

19. Markofski 2015; Marti and Ganiel 2014, 5.

20. Bender 2010.

21. Edgell 2005.

References

Acevedo, Gabriel A., and Ali R. Chaudhary. 2015. "Religion, Cultural Clash, and Muslim American Attitudes About Politically Motivated Violence." *Journal for the Scientific Study of Religion* 54, no. 2: 242–60.

Allport, Gordon. 1979. *The Nature of Prejudice*. 25th anniversary ed. Cambridge, MA: Perseus Books.

Ammerman, Nancy Tatom. 2005. *Pillars of Faith: American Congregations and Their Partners*. Berkeley: University of California Press.

———. 2006. *Everyday Religion: Observing Modern Religious Lives*. New York: Oxford University Press.

Anderson, Shawna L., Jessica Hamar Martinez, Catherine Hoegeman, Gary Adler, and Mark Chaves. 2008. "Dearly Departed: How Often Do Congregations Close?" *Journal for the Scientific Study of Religion* 47, no. 2: 321–28.

Andrews, Kenneth T. 2002. "Movement-Countermovement Dynamics and the Emergence of New Institutions: The Case of 'White Flight' Schools in Mississippi." *Social Forces* 80, no. 3: 911–36.

Andrews, Kenneth T., Kraig Beyerlein, and Tuneka Tucker Farnum. 2016. "The Legitimacy of Protest: Explaining White Southerners' Attitudes Toward the Civil Rights Movement." *Social Forces* 94, no. 3: 1021–44.

Andrews, Kenneth T., and Charles Seguin. 2015. "Group Threat and Policy Change: The Spatial Dynamics of Prohibition Politics, 1890–1919." *American Journal of Sociology* 121, no. 2: 475–510.

"Arab Americans: Demographics." 2005. Arab American Institute. Accessed August 1, 2019. https://web.archive.org/web/20060601221810/http://www .aaiusa.org/arab-americans/22/demographics.

Argue, Amy, David R. Johnson, and Lynn K. White. 1999. "Age and Religiosity: Evidence from a Three-Wave Panel Analysis." *Journal for the Scientific Study of Religion* 38, no. 3: 423–35.

Asi, Maryam, and Daniel Beaulieu. 2013. "Arab Households in the United States: 2006–2010." American Community Survey Briefs US Census Bureau. https://www2.census.gov/library/publications/2013/acs/acsbr10-20.pdf.

Avishai, Orit. 2008. "'Doing Religion' in a Secular World: Women in Conservative Religions and the Question of Agency." *Gender and Society* 22, no. 4: 409–33.

———. 2016. "Gender." In *Handbook of Religion and Society*, edited by David Yamane, 373–94. Switzerland: Springer International Publishing.

Avishai, Orit, Afshan Jafar, and Rachel Rinaldo. 2015. "A Gender Lens on Religion." *Gender & Society* 29, no. 1: 5–25.

Axtell, James. 1981. *The European and the Indian: Essays in the Ethnohistory of Colonial North America*. New York: Oxford University Press.

Bagby, Ihsan. 2012. "The American Mosque 2011: Basic Characteristics of the American Mosque; Attitudes of Mosque Leaders." Report Number 1 from the US Mosque Study 2011 CAIR. http://faithcommunitiestoday.org/sites /faithcommunitiestoday.org/files/The%20American%20Mosque%20 2011%20web.pdf.

Bail, Christopher. 2014. *Terrified: How Anti-Muslim Fringe Organizations Became Mainstream*. Princeton, NJ: Princeton University Press.

Balmer, Randall. 2007. *Thy Kingdom Come: How the Religious Right Distorts Faith and Threatens America*. New York: Basic Books.

Balmer, Randall, Kate Bowler, Anthea Butler, Maura Jane Farrelly, Wes Markofski, Robert Orsi, Jerry Z. Park, James Clark Davidson, Matthew Avery Sutton, and Grace Yukich. 2017. "Forum: Studying Religion in the Age of Trump." *Religion and American Culture* 27, no. 1: 2–56.

Bankston, Carl L., and Min Zhou. 2000. "De Facto Congregationalism and Socioeconomic Mobility in Laotian and Vietnamese Immigrant Communities: A Study of Religious Institutions and Economic Change." *Review of Religious Research* 41, no. 4: 453–70.

Barker, Philip. 2009. *Religious Nationalism in Modern Europe: If God Be for Us*. London: Routledge.

Barnes, Sandra L. 2005. "Black Church Culture and Community Action." *Social Forces* 84, no. 2: 967–94.

———. 2006. "Whosoever Will Let Her Come: Social Activism and Gender Inclusivity in the Black Church." *Journal for the Scientific Study of Religion* 45, no. 3: 371–87.

———. 2010. *Black Megachurch Culture: Models for Education and Empowerment*. Black Studies and Critical Thinking, vol. 3. New York: Peter Lang.

Bellah, Robert N. 1964. "Religious Evolution." *American Sociological Review* 29, no. 3: 358–74.

Bender, Courtney. 2010. *The New Metaphysicals: Spirituality and the American Religious Imagination*. Chicago: University of Chicago Press.

Bengtson, Vern L., Norella M. Putney, and Susan Harris. 2013. *Families and Faith: How Religion Is Passed down across Generations*. New York: Oxford University Press.

Bengtson, Vern L., R. David Hayward, Phil Zuckerman, and Merril Silverstein. 2018. "Bringing Up Nones: Intergenerational Influences and Cohort Trends." *Journal for the Scientific Study of Religion* 57, no. 2: 258–75.

Berger, Peter L. 1967. *The Sacred Canopy: Elements of a Sociological Theory of Religion*. New York: Doubleday & Co.

Berger, Peter L., Grace Davie, and Effie Fokas. 2008. *Religious America, Secular Europe? A Theme and Variation*. Aldershot: Ashgate Publishing Limited.

Beyerlein, Kraig. 2004. "Specifying the Impact of Conservative Protestantism on Educational Attainment." *Journal for the Scientific Study of Religion* 43, no. 4: 505–18.

Bibby, Reginald W. 1997. "Going, Going, Gone: The Impact of Geographical Mobility on Religious Involvement." *Review of Religious Research* 38, no. 4: 289–307.

Bibby, Reginald W., and Merlin B. Brinkerhoff. 1994. "Circulation of the Saints 1966–1990: New Data, New Reflections." *Journal for the Scientific Study of Religion* 33, no. 3: 273–80.

Bird, Warren. n.d. "The World's Largest Churches: A Country-by-Country List of Global Megachurches." Leadership Network. Accessed January 20, 2020. https://leadnet.org/world/.

Bloom, Pazit Ben-Nun, Gizem Arikan, and Marie Courtemanche. 2015. "Religious Social Identity, Religious Belief, and Anti-Immigration Sentiment." *American Political Science Review* 109, no. 2: 203–21.

"Blue Law." n.d. Encyclopedia Brittanica Online. Accessed September 13, 2018. https://www.britannica.com/topic/blue-law.

Boddie, Stephanie Clinton, Rebekah P. Massengill, and Anne Fengyan Shi. 2002. "Did the Religious Group Socioeconomic Ranking Change Leading into the Great Recession?" In *Religion, Work, and Inequality*, edited by Lisa A. Keister, John McCarthy, and Roger Finke, 27–48. Research in the Sociology of Work, vol. 23. Bingley: Emerald Publishing Limited.

Brauer, Simon G. 2017. "How Many Congregations Are There? Updating a Survey-Based Estimate." *Journal for the Scientific Study of Religion* 56, no. 2: 438–48.

Braunstein, Ruth. 2017a. *Prophets and Patriots: Faith in Democracy across the Political Divide*. Berkeley: University of California Press.

———. 2017b. "Muslims as Outsiders, Enemies, and Others: The 2016 Presidential Election and the Politics of Religious Exclusion." *American Journal of Cultural Sociology* 5, no. 3: 355–72.

———. 2018. "A (More) Perfect Union? Religion, Politics, and Competing Stories of America." *Sociology of Religion* 79, no. 2: 172–95.

Brooks, Clem, and Jeff Manza. 1997. "Social Cleavages and Political Alignments: U.S. Presidential Elections, 1960 to 1992." *American Sociological Review* 62, no. 6: 937–46.

Brown, R. Khari, Robert Joseph Taylor, and Linda M. Chatters. 2015. "Race/Ethnic and Social-Demographic Correlates of Religious Non-Involvement in America: Findings from Three National Surveys." *Journal of Black Studies* 46, no. 4: 335–62.

Burge, Ryan. 2019. "By Their Tweets You Will Know Them: The Democrats' Continuing God Gap." *Religion News Service*, August 30, 2019. https://religionnews.com/2019/08/30/by-their-tweets-you-will-know -them-the-democrats-continuing-god-gap/.

Bushman, Richard Lyman. 2007. *Joseph Smith: Rough Stone Rolling*. New York: Vintage Books.

Butler, Jon, Grant Wacker, and Randall Balmer. 2008. *Religion in American Life: A Short History*. 2nd ed. New York: Oxford University Press.

Cadge, Wendy. 2008. "De Facto Congregationalism and the Religious Organizations of Post-1965 Immigrants to the United States." *Journal of the American Academy of Religion* 76, no. 2: 344–74.

Cadge, Wendy, and Elaine Howard Ecklund. 2007. "Immigration and Religion." *Annual Review of Sociology* 33, no. 1: 359–79.

Camarota, Steven A., and Karen Zeigler. 2018. "Central American Immigrant Population Increased Nearly 28-Fold since 1970." Center for Immigration Studies. Accessed August 1, 2019. https://cis.org/sites/default/files/2018-11 /central-america-nov-18_0.pdf.

Capps, Walter H. 1990. *The New Religious Right: Piety, Patriotism, and Politics*. Columbia, SC: University of South Carolina Press.

Casanova, José. 2007. "Immigration and the New Religious Pluralism: A European Union/United States Comparison." In *Democracy and the New Religious Pluralism*, edited by Thomas Banchoff, 59–84. New York: Oxford University Press.

Cavendish, James C. 2002. "Church-Based Community Activism: A Comparison of Black and White Catholic Congregations." *Journal for the Scientific Study of Religion* 39, no. 1: 64–77.

Chappell, David. 1994. *Inside Agitators: White Southerners in the Civil Rights Movement*. Baltimore: Johns Hopkins University Press.

———. 2004. *A Stone of Hope: Prophetic Religion and the Death of Jim Crow*. Chapel Hill, NC: University of North Carolina Press.

Chatters, Linda M., Robert J. Taylor, Kai M. Bullard, and James S. Jackson. 2009. "Race and Ethnic Differences in Religious Involvement: African Americans, Caribbean Blacks and Non-Hispanic Whites." *Ethnic and Racial Studies* 32, no. 7: 1143–63.

Chaves, Mark. 2004. *Congregations in America*. Cambridge, MA: Harvard University Press.

———. 2006. "All Creatures Great and Small: Megachurches in Context." *Review of Religious Research* 47, no. 4: 329–46.

———. 2011. *American Religion: Contemporary Trends*. Princeton, NJ: Princeton University Press.

———. 2017. *American Religion: Contemporary Trends*. 2nd ed. Princeton, NJ: Princeton University Press.

Chaves, Mark, and Shawna L. Anderson. 2014. "Changing American Congregations: Findings from the Third Wave of the National Congregations Study." *Journal for the Scientific Study of Religion* 53, no. 4: 676–86.

Chaves, Mark, and Alison Eagle. 2015. "Religious Congregations in 21st Century America: A Report from the National Congregations Study." Durham, NC: Department of Sociology, Duke University. http://www.soc.duke.edu/natcong/Docs/NCSIII_report_final.pdf.

Chaves, Mark, and Philip S. Gorski. 2001. "Religious Pluralism and Religious Participation." *Annual Review of Sociology* 27, no. 1: 261–81.

Chaves, Mark, and William Tsitsos. 2001. "Congregations and Social Services: What They Do, How They Do It, and with Whom." *Nonprofit and Voluntary Sector Quarterly* 30, no. 4: 660–83.

Christerson, Brad, and Michael O. Emerson. 2003. "The Costs of Diversity in Religious Organizations: An In-Depth Case Study." *Sociology of Religion* 64, no. 2: 163–81.

Cimino, Richard. 2005. "'No God in Common:' American Evangelical Discourse on Islam after 9/11." *Review of Religious Research* 47, no. 2: 162–74.

Cobb, Ryon J., Samuel L. Perry, and Kevin D. Dougherty. 2015. "United by Faith? Race/Ethnicity, Congregational Diversity, and Explanations of Racial Inequality." *Sociology of Religion* 76, no. 2: 177–98.

Cobb, Ryon J., Dilara K. Üsküp, and Steven T. Jefferson. 2017. "Congregational Composition and Explanations for Racial Inequality Among Black Religious Affiliates." *Race and Social Problems* 9, no. 2: 163–69.

Cohen, Philip N. 2014. "This Word 'Generation,' I Do Not Think It Means What You Think It Means." Family Inequality. October 7, 2014. https://familyinequality.wordpress.com/2014/10/07/this-word-generation-i-do-not-think-it-means-what-you-think-it-meants/

Collett, Jessica L., and Omar Lizardo. 2009. "A Power-Control Theory of Gender and Religiosity." *Journal for the Scientific Study of Religion* 48, no. 2: 213–31.

Cooke, Thomas J. 2011. "It Is Not Just the Economy: Declining Migration and the Rise of Secular Rootedness." *Population, Space and Place* 17, no. 3: 193–203.

———. 2013. "Internal Migration in Decline." *Professional Geographer* 65, no. 4: 664–75.

Cornwall, Marie. 2009. "Reifying Sex Difference Isn't the Answer: Gendering Processes, Risk, and Religiosity." *Journal for the Scientific Study of Religion* 48, no. 2: 252–55.

Cressler, Matthew J. 2017. *Authentically Black and Truly Catholic: The Rise of Black Catholicism in the Great Migration.* New York: New York University Press.

Daniels, Roger. 1977. *The Politics of Prejudice: The Anti-Japanese Movement in California and the Struggle for Japanese Exclusion.* 2nd ed. Berkeley: University of California Press.

———. 2004. *Guarding the Golden Door: American Immigration Policy and Immigrants since 1882.* New York: Hill and Wang.

D'Antonio, William V., and Dean R. Hoge. 2006. "The American Experience of Religious Disestablishment and Pluralism." *Social Compass* 53, no. 3: 345–56.

Darnell, Alfred, and Darren E. Sherkat. 1997. "The Impact of Protestant Fundamentalism on Educational Attainment." *American Sociological Review* 62, no. 2: 306–15.

Davidson, James, and Ralph E. Pyle. 2011. *Ranking Faiths: Religious Stratification in America.* Lanham, MD: Rowman & Littlefield Publishers.

Day, Katie. 2001. "The Construction of Political Strategies among African American Clergy." In *Christian Clergy in American Politics,* edited by Sue Crawford and Laura R. Olson, 85–103. Baltimore: Johns Hopkins University Press.

De Vaus, David A. 1984. "Workforce Participation and Sex Differences in Church Attendance." *Review of Religious Research* 25, no. 3: 247–56.

Delehanty, Jack. 2018. "The Emotional Management of Progressive Religious Mobilization." *Sociology of Religion* 79, no. 2: 248–72.

Dillon, Michele, and Paul Wink. 2007. *In the Course of a Lifetime: Tracing Religious Belief, Practice, and Change.* Berkeley: University of California Press.

Dimock, Michael. 2019. "Defining Generations: Where Millennials End and Generation Z Begins." Pew Research Center. January 17, 2019. https://www.pewresearch.org/fact-tank/2019/01/17/where-millennials-end-and-generation-z-begins/.

Dougherty, Kevin D., and Kimberly R. Huyser. 2008. "Racially Diverse Congregations: Organizational Identity and the Accommodation of Differences." *Journal for the Scientific Study of Religion* 47, no. 1: 23–44.

Dougherty, Kevin D., Brandon C. Martinez, and Gerardo Marti. 2016. "Congregational Diversity and Attendance in a Mainline Protestant Denomination." *Journal for the Scientific Study of Religion* 54, no. 4: 668–83.

Durkheim, Emile. 1995. *The Elementary Forms of Religious Life*. Translated by Karen E. Fields. New York: Simon & Schuster.

Eagle, David E. 2012. "Mega, Medium, and Mini: Size and the Socioeconomic Status Composition of American Protestant Churches." In *Religion, Work and Inequality*, edited by Lisa A. Keister, John McCarthy, and Roger Finke, 281–309. Research in the Sociology of Work, vol. 23. Bingley: Emerald Group Publishing Limited.

———. 2015. "Historicizing the Megachurch." *Journal of Social History* 48, no. 3: 589–604.

———. 2016. "The Negative Relationship between Size and the Probability of Weekly Attendance in Churches in the United States." *Socius* 2: 1–10.

Ebaugh, Helen Rose. 2003. "Religion and the New Immigrants." In *Handbook of the Sociology of Religion*, edited by Michele Dillon, 225–39. New York: Cambridge University Press.

Ebaugh, Helen Rose, and Janet Saltzman Chafetz. 2000. "Dilemmas of Language in Immigrant Congregations: The Tie That Binds or the Tower of Babel?" *Review of Religious Research* 41, no. 4: 432–52.

Ecklund, Elaine Howard. 2005. "Models of Civic Responsibility: Korean Americans in Congregations with Different Ethnic Compositions." *Journal for the Scientific Study of Religion* 44, no. 1: 15–28.

Edgell, Penny. 2005. *Religion and Family in a Changing Society*. Princeton, NJ: Princeton University Press.

———. 2012. "A Cultural Sociology of Religion: New Directions." Annual Review of Sociology 38: 247–65.

———. 2017. "An Agenda for Research on American Religion in Light of the 2016 Election." *Sociology of Religion* 78, no. 1: 1–8.

Edgell, Penny, Joseph Gerteis, and Douglas Hartmann. 2006. "Atheists as 'Other': Moral Boundaries and Cultural Membership in American Society." *American Sociological Review* 71, no. 2: 211–34.

Edgell, Penny, Douglas Hartmann, Evan Stewart, and Joseph Gerteis. 2016. "Atheists and Other Cultural Outsiders: Moral Boundaries and the Non-Religious in the United States." *Social Forces* 95, no. 2: 607–38.

Edwards, Korie L. 2008a. *The Elusive Dream: The Power of Race in Interracial Churches*. New York: Oxford University Press.

———. 2008b. "Bring Race to the Center: The Importance of Race in Racially Diverse Religious Organizations." *Journal for the Scientific Study of Religion* 47, no. 1: 5–9.

———. 2009. "Race, Religion, and Worship: Are Contemporary African-American Worship Practices Distinct?" *Journal for the Scientific Study of Religion* 48, no. 1: 30–52.

Edwards, Korie L., Brad Christerson, and Michael O. Emerson. 2013. "Race, Religious Organizations, and Integration." *Annual Review of Sociology* 39, no. 1: 211–28.

Elder, Glen. 1974. *Children of the Great Depression: Social Change in Life Experience*. Chicago: University of Chicago Press.

Ellingson, Stephen. 2009. "The Rise of the Megachurches and Changes in Religious Culture: Review Article." *Sociology Compass* 3, no. 1: 16–30.

———. 2010. "New Research on Megachurches." In *The New Blackwell Companion to the Sociology of Religion*, edited by Bryan S. Turner, 247–66. Chichester: John Wiley & Sons Ltd.

Ellis, Rachel. 2018. "'It's Not Equality': How Race, Class, and Gender Construct the Normative Religious Self among Female Prisoners." *Social Inclusion* 6, no. 2: 181–91.

Ellison, Christopher G., Neal M. Krause, Bryan C. Shepherd, and Mark A. Chaves. 2009. "Size, Conflict, and Opportunities for Interaction: Congregational Effects on Members' Anticipated Support and Negative Interaction." *Journal for the Scientific Study of Religion* 48, no. 1: 1–15.

Ellison, Christopher G., and Darren E. Sherkat. 1990. "Patterns of Religious Mobility among Black Americans." *Sociological Quarterly* 31, no. 4: 551–68.

———. 1995. "The 'Semi-Involuntary Institution' Revisited: Regional Variations in Church Participation among Black Americans." *Social Forces* 73, no. 4: 1415–37.

Emerson, Michael O. 2008. "Introduction: Why a Forum on Racially and Ethnically Diverse Congregations?" *Journal for the Scientific Study of Religion* 47, no. 1: 1–4.

Emerson, Michael O., and Karen Chai Kim. 2003. "Multiracial Congregations: An Analysis of Their Development and a Typology." *Journal for the Scientific Study of Religion* 42, no. 2: 217–27.

Emerson, Michael O., Elizabeth Korver-Glenn, and Kiara W. Douds. 2015. "Studying Race and Religion: A Critical Assessment." *Sociology of Race and Ethnicity* 1, no. 3: 349–59.

Emerson, Michael O., and Christian Smith. 2001. *Divided by Faith: Evangelical Religion and the Problem of Race in America*. New York: Oxford University Press.

Eppsteiner, Holly Straut, and Jacqueline Hagan. 2016. "Religion as Psychological, Spiritual, and Social Support in the Migration Undertaking." *Intersec-*

tions of Religion and Migration Religion and Global Migrations New York: Palgrave Macmillan.

"Exploring Congregations in America." n.d. Association of Religion Data Archives. Accessed January 20, 2020. http://www.thearda.com /learningcenter/modules/module8.asp.

Feigelman, William, Bernard S. Gorman, and Joseph A. Varacalli. 1991. "The Social Characteristics of Black Catholics." *Sociology and Social Research* 75, no. 3: 133–43.

Fetzer, Joel. 2000. *Public Attitudes toward Immigration in the United States, France, and Germany.* New York: Cambridge University Press.

Findlay, James. 1993. *Church People in the Struggle: The National Council of Churches and the Black Freedom Movement, 1950–1970.* New York: Oxford University Press.

Finke, Roger. 1989. "Demographics of Religious Participation: An Ecological Approach, 1850–1980." *Journal for the Scientific Study of Religion* 28, no. 1: 45–58.

———. 1990. "Religious Deregulation: Origins and Consequences." *Journal of Church and State* 32, no. 3: 609–26.

Finke, Roger, and Rodney Stark. 2005. *The Churching of America, 1776–2005.* New Brunswick, NJ: Rutgers University Press.

Fiorina, Morris P. 2016. "Has the American Public Polarized?" *Hoover Institution Essays on Contemporary American Politics* 2 (September): 1–24.

Fitzgerald, Scott T., and Jennifer L. Glass. 2014. "Conservative Protestants, Normative Pathways, and Adult Attainment." In *Religion and Inequality in America: Research and Theory on Religion's Role in Stratification,* edited by Lisa A. Keister and Darren E. Sherkat, 97–118. New York: Cambridge University Press.

Flory, Richard, and Donald E. Miller. 2008. *Finding Faith: The Spiritual Quest of the Post-Boomer Generation.* New Brunswick, NJ: Rutgers University Press.

Fowler, Robert, Kevin R. den Dulk, Allen D. Hertzke, and Laura R. Olson. 2014. *Religion and Politics in America: Faith, Culture, and Strategic Choices.* 5th ed. Boulder, CO: Westview Press.

Freeland, Gregory. 2010. "Negotiating Place, Space and Borders: The New Sanctuary Movement." *Latino Studies* 8, no. 4: 485–508.

Frey, William H. 2018. *Diversity Explosion: How New Racial Demographics Are Remaking America.* Washington, DC: Brookings Institution Press.

Friedland, Michael. 1998. *Lift up Your Voice like a Trumpet: White Clergy and the Civil Rights and Antiwar Movements, 1954–1973.* Chapel Hill, NC: University of North Carolina Press.

Fugita, Stephen, and Marilyn Fernandez. 2002. "Religion and Japanese Americans' Views of Their World War II Incarceration." *Journal of Asian American Studies* 5, no. 2: 113–37.

Gallup, George Jr. 1999. *Surveying the Religious Landscape: Trends in U.S. Beliefs.* Harrisburg, PA: Morehouse Publishing.

Garces-Foley, Kathleen. 2008. "Comparing Catholic and Evangelical Integration Efforts." *Journal for the Scientific Study of Religion* 47, no. 1: 17–22.

Geertz, Clifford. 1973. *The Interpretation of Cultures.* New York: Basic Books.

George, Linda K., Christopher G. Ellison, and David B. Larson. 2002. "Explaining the Relationships Between Religious Involvement and Health." *Psychological Inquiry* 13, no. 3: 190–200.

Goodman, William R., Jr. and James J. H. Price. 1981. *Jerry Falwell: An Unauthorized Profile.* Lynchburg, VA: Paris & Associates.

Gorman, Brandon. 2018. "The Myth of the Secular–Islamist Divide in Muslim Politics: Evidence from Tunisia." *Current Sociology* 66, no. 1: 145–64.

Gorski, Philip S. 2017. "Why Evangelicals Voted for Trump: A Critical Cultural Sociology." *American Journal of Cultural Sociology* 5, no. 3: 338–54.

Gorski, Philip S., and Ateş Altınordu. 2008. "After Secularization?" *Annual Review of Sociology* 34, no. 1: 55–85.

Granovetter, Mark S. 1973. "The Strength of Weak Ties." *American Journal of Sociology* 78, no. 6: 1360–80.

Grant, J. Tobin. 2008. "Measuring Aggregate Religiosity in the United States, 1952–2005." *Sociological Spectrum* 28, no. 5: 460–76.

Gray, Mark, Mary Gautier, and Thomas Gaunt. 2014. "Cultural Diversity in the Catholic Church in the United States." Washington, DC: Center for Applied Research in the Apostolate at Georgetown University. http://www.usccb.org/issues-and-action/cultural-diversity/upload/cultural-diversity-cara-report-phase-1.pdf.

Greeley, Andrew. 2003. *Religion in Europe at the End of the Second Millennium: A Sociological Profile.* New Brunswick, NJ: Transaction Publishers.

Greeley, Andrew M., and Michael Hout. 1999. "Americans' Increasing Belief in Life after Death: Religious Competition and Acculturation." *American Sociological Review* 64, no. 6: 813–35.

Griffith, R. Marie. 2017. *Moral Combat: How Sex Divided American Christians and Fractured American Politics.* Basic Books.

Gusfield, Joseph R. 1986. *Symbolic Crusade: Status Politics and the American Temperance Movement.* Champaign, IL: University of Illinois Press.

Hackett, Conrad, Marcin Stonawski, Michaela Potančoková, Brian J. Grim, and Vegard Skirbekk. 2015. "The Future Size of Religiously Affiliated and Unaffiliated Populations." *Demographic Research* 32: 829–42.

Hadaway, C. Kirk and Penny Long Marler. 2006. "Growth and Decline in the Mainline." In *Faith in America: Changes, Challenges, New Directions.* Vol. 1, *Organized Religion Today,* edited by C. H. Lippy, 1–24. Westport, CT: Praeger.

Hadaway, C. Kirk, Penny Long Marler, and Mark Chaves. 1993. "What the Polls Don't Show: A Closer Look at U.S. Church Attendance." *American Sociological Review* 58, no. 6: 741–52.

Hagan, Jacqueline. 2008. *Migration Miracle: Faith, Hope, and Meaning on the Undocumented Journey.* Cambridge, MA: Harvard University Press.

Hagan, Jacqueline, and Helen Rose Ebaugh. 2003. "Calling upon the Sacred: Migrants' Use of Religion in the Migration Process." *International Migration Review* 37, no. 4: 1145–62.

Hayward, R. David, and Neal Krause. 2013. "Patterns of Change in Religious Service Attendance across the Life Course: Evidence from a 34-Year Longitudinal Study." *Social Science Research* 42, no. 6: 1480–89.

———. 2015. "Aging, Social Developmental, and Cultural Factors in Changing Patterns of Religious Involvement over a 32-Year Period: An Age–Period–Cohort Analysis of 80 Countries." *Journal of Cross-Cultural Psychology* 46, no. 8: 979–95.

Hill, Peter C., and Kenneth I. Pargament. 2003. "Advances in the Conceptualization and Measurement of Religion and Spirituality: Implications for Physical and Mental Health Research." *American Psychologist* 58, no. 1: 64–74.

Hill, Peter C., Kenneth I Pargament, Ralph W. Hood, Michael E. McCullough Jr., James P. Swyers, David B. Larson, and Brian J. Zinnbauer. 2000. "Conceptualizing Religion and Spirituality: Points of Commonality, Points of Departure." *Journal for the Theory of Social Behaviour* 30, no. 1: 51–77.

Hipple, Steven F. 2016. "Labor Force Participation: What Has Happened since the Peak?" Monthly Labor Review US Bureau of Labor Statistics. https://www.bls.gov/opub/mlr/2016/article/labor-force-participation-what-has-happened-since-the-peak.htm.

Hirschman, Charles. 2006. "The Role of Religion in the Origins and Adaptation of Immigrant Groups in the United States." *International Migration Review* 38, no. 3: 1206–33.

Hoffmann, John P. 2009. "Gender, Risk, and Religiousness: Can Power Control Provide the Theory?" *Journal for the Scientific Study of Religion* 48, no. 2: 232–40.

Hoffmann, John P., and Sherrie Mills Johnson. 2005. "Attitudes toward Abortion among Religious Traditions in the United States: Change or Continuity?" *Sociology of Religion* 66, no. 2: 161–82.

Hoffmann, John P., and Alan S. Miller. 1997. "Social and Political Attitudes among Religious Groups: Convergence and Divergence over Time." *Journal for the Scientific Study of Religion* 36, no. 1: 52–70.

Hornick, Ed. 2008. "Obama, McCain Talk Issues at Pastor's Forum." *CNN.Com.* August 17, 2008. http://www.cnn.com/2008/POLITICS/08/16/warren.forum/.

Hout, Michael. 2016. "Saint Peter's Leaky Boat: Falling Intergenerational Persistence among U.S.-Born Catholics since 1974." *Sociology of Religion* 77, no. 1: 1–17.

———. 2017a. "Religious Ambivalence, Liminality, and the Increase of No Religious Preference in the United States, 2006–2014." *Journal for the Scientific Study of Religion* 56, no. 1: 52–63.

———. 2017b. "American Religion, All or Nothing at All." *Contexts* 16, no. 4: 78–80.

Hout, Michael, and Claude S. Fischer. 2002. "Why More Americans Have No Religious Preference: Politics and Generations." *American Sociological Review* 67, no. 2: 165–90.

———. 2014. "Explaining Why More Americans Have No Religious Preference: Political Backlash and Generational Succession, 1987–2012." *Sociological Science* 1: 423–47.

Hout, Michael, Andrew Greeley, and Melissa J. Wilde. 2001. "The Demographic Imperative in Religious Change in the United States." *American Journal of Sociology* 107, no. 2: 468–500.

Hummer, Robert A., Richard G. Rogers, Charles B. Nam, and Christopher G. Ellison. 1999. "Religious Involvement and U.S. Adult Mortality." *Demography* 36, no. 2: 273–85.

Hunt, Larry L. 1998. "Religious Affiliation among Blacks in the United States: Black Catholic Status Advantages Revisited." *Social Science Quarterly* 79, no. 1: 170–92.

Hunt, Larry L., and Janet G. Hunt. 1978. "Black Catholicism and Occupational Status in Northern Cities." *Social Science Quarterly* 58, no. 4: 657–70.

Hunt, Larry L., and Matthew O. Hunt. 1999. "Regional Patterns of African American Church Attendance: Revisiting the Semi-Involuntary Thesis." *Social Forces* 78, no. 2: 779–91.

———. 2001. "Race, Region, and Religious Involvement: A Comparative Study of Whites and African Americans." *Social Forces* 80, no. 2: 605–31.

Hunter, James D. 1991. *Culture Wars: The Struggle to Define America.* New York: Basic Books.

Huntington, Samuel P. 1993. "The Clash of Civilizations?" *Foreign Affairs* 72, no. 3: 22–49.

———. 1996. *The Clash of Civilizations and the Remaking of World Order.* New York: Simon & Schuster.

Hurh, Won Moo, and Kwang Chung Kim. 1990. "Religious Participation of Korean Immigrants in the United States." *Journal for the Scientific Study of Religion* 29, no. 1: 19–34.

Iannaccone, Laurence R. 1994. "Why Strict Churches Are Strong." *American Journal of Sociology* 99, no. 5: 1180–1211.

Iannaccone, Laurence R., and Michael D. Makowsky. 2007. "Accidental Atheists? Agent-Based Explanations for the Persistence of Religious Regionalism." *Journal for the Scientific Study of Religion* 46, no. 1: 1–16.

Ingersoll-Dayton, Berit, Neal Krause, and David Morgan. 2002. "Religious Trajectories and Transitions Over the Life Course." *International Journal of Aging and Human Development* 55, no. 1: 51–70.

James, Angela. 2001. "Making Sense of Race and Racial Classification." *Race and Society* 4, no. 2: 235–47.

Jasso, Guillermina, Douglas S. Massey, and Mark R. Rosenzweig. 2003. "Exploring the Religious Preference of Recent Immigrants to the United States: Evidence from the New Immigrant Survey Pilot." In *Religion and Immigration: Christian, Jewish, and Muslim Experiences in the United States*, edited by John Esposito, Yvonne Yazbeck Haddad, and Jane I. Smith, 217–53. Walnut Creek, CA: AltaMira Press.

Jelen, Ted G., and Clyde Wilcox. 2002. *Religion and Politics in Comparative Perspective: The One, The Few, and The Many.* Cambridge: Cambridge University Press.

Jenkins, Jack. 2019. "In Polarized Washington, a Democrat Anchors Bipartisan Friendships in Faith." Religion News Service. January 29, 2019. https://religionnews.com/2019/01/29/in-polarized-washington-a-democrat-anchors-bipartisan-friendships-in-faith/.

Juergensmeyer, Mark. 2017a. *Terror in the Mind of God: The Global Rise of Religious Violence.* 4th ed. Berkeley: University of California Press.

———. 2017b. "The Global Rise of Religious Nationalism." In *Current Issues in Law and Religion*, vol. 4, edited by Silvio Ferrari and Rinaldo Cristofori, 41–52. London: Routledge..

Kaplan, Greg, and Sam Schulhofer-Wohl. 2012. "Interstate Migration Has Fallen Less Than You Think: Consequences of Hot Deck Imputation in the Current Population Survey." *Demography* 49, no. 3: 1061–74.

Karnes, Kimberly, Wayne McIntosh, Irwin L. Morris, and Shanna Pearson Merkowitz. 2007. "Mighty Fortresses: Explaining the Spatial Distribution of American Megachurches." *Journal for the Scientific Study of Religion* 46, no. 2: 261–68.

Kaufmann, Eric, Anne Goujon, and Vegard Skirbekk. 2012. "The End of Secularization in Europe? A Socio-Demographic Perspective." *Sociology of Religion* 73, no. 1: 69–91.

Keister, Lisa A. 2003. "Religion and Wealth: The Role of Religious Affiliation and Participation in Early Adult Asset Accumulation." *Social Forces* 82, no. 1: 175–207.

———. 2008. "Conservative Protestants and Wealth: How Religion Perpetuates Asset Poverty." *American Journal of Sociology* 113, no. 5: 1237–71.

Keister, Lisa A., and Darren E. Sherkat. 2014. *Religion and Inequality in America: Research and Theory on Religion's Role in Stratification.* New York: Cambridge University Press.

Kennedy, Edward M. 1966. "The Immigration Act of 1965." *Annals of the American Academy of Political and Social Science* 367, no. 1: 137–49.

King, Martin Luther, Jr. 1960. Interview transcript, "Meet the Press." April 17, 1960. The Martin Luther King, Jr. Research and Education Institute, Stanford University. Accessed January 20, 2020. https://kinginstitute .stanford.edu/king-papers/documents/interview-meet-press.

Kosmin, Barry A., and Ariela Keysar. 2009. "American Religious Identity Survey: Summary Report." Accessed July 26, 2018. http://commons.trincoll .edu/aris/files/2011/08/ARIS_Report_2008.pdf.

Kosmin, Barry A., Ariela Keysar, Ryan Cragun, and Juhem Navarro-Rivera. 2009. "American Nones: The Profile of the No Religion Population." Hartford, CT: Trinity College Program on Public Values. https://commons .trincoll.edu/aris/publications/2008-2/american-nones-the-profile-of-the-no -religion-population/

Kosmin, Barry A., Ariela Keysar, and Nava Lerer. 1992. "Secular Education and the Religious Profile of Contemporary Black and White Americans." *Journal for the Scientific Study of Religion* 31, no. 4: 523–32.

Lajevardi, Nazita, and Kassra A. R. Oskooii. 2018. "Old-Fashioned Racism, Contemporary Islamophobia, and the Isolation of Muslim Americans in the Age of Trump." *Journal of Race, Ethnicity, and Politics* 3, no. 1: 112–52.

Lamont, Michèle, and Virág Molnár. 2002. "The Study of Boundaries in the Social Sciences." *Annual Review of Sociology* 28, no. 1: 167–95.

Latterell, Justin. 2011. "In God We Trust: Abraham Lincoln and America's Deathbed Repentance." *Political Theology* 12, no. 4: 594–607.

Leamaster, Reid J. 2012. "A Research Note on English-Speaking Buddhists in the United States." *Journal for the Scientific Study of Religion* 51, no. 1: 143–55.

Leavy, Zad, and Alan F. Charles. 1967. "California's New Therapeutic Abortion Act: An Analysis and Guide to Medical and Legal Procedure." *UCLA Law Review* 15: 1–31.

Lee, Bo Hyeong J., and Lisa D. Pearce. 2019. "Understanding Why Religious Involvement's Relationship with Education Varies by Social Class." *Journal of Research on Adolescence* 29, no. 2: 369–89.

Lehrer, Evelyn L. 2004. "Religion as a Determinant of Economic and Demographic Behavior in the United States." *Population and Development Review* 30, no. 4: 707–26.

———. 1999. "Religion as a Determinant of Educational Attainment: An Economic Perspective." *Social Science Research* 28, no. 4: 358–79.

Lien, Pei-te, and Tony Carnes. 2004. "The Religious Demography of Asian American Boundary Crossing." In *Asian American Religions: The Making and Remaking of Borders and Boundaries*, edited by Tony Carnes and Fenggang Yang, 38–53. New York: New York University Press.

Lin, Nan. 1999. "Social Networks and Status Attainment." *Annual Review of Sociology* 25: 467–87.

Lincoln, C. Eric, and Lawrence H. Mamiya. 1990. *The Black Church in the African-American Experience*. Durham, NC: Duke University Press.

Lindsay, D. Michael. 2007. *Faith in the Halls of Power: How Evangelicals Joined the American Elite*. New York: Oxford University Press.

Lizardo, Omar, and Jessica L. Collett. 2009. "Rescuing the Baby from the Bathwater: Continuing the Conversation on Gender, Risk, and Religiosity." *Journal for the Scientific Study of Religion* 48, no. 2: 256–59.

Loveland, Anne C., and Otis B. Wheeler. 2003. *From Meetinghouse to Megachurch: A Material and Cultural History*. Columbia, MO: University of Missouri Press.

Mahoney, Annette, Kenneth I. Pargament, Nalini Tarakeshwar, and Aaron B. Swank. 2001. "Religion in the Home in the 1980s and 1990s: A Meta-Analytic Review and Conceptual Analysis of Links between Religion, Marriage, and Parenting." *Journal of Family Psychology* 15, no. 4: 559–96.

Manza, Jeff, and Clem Brooks. 1997. "The Religious Factor in U.S. Presidential Elections, 1960–1992." *American Journal of Sociology* 103, no. 1: 38–81.

Markofski, Wes. 2015. *New Monasticism and the Transformation of American Evangelicalism*. New York: Oxford University Press.

Marti, Gerardo. 2005. *A Mosaic of Believers: Diversity and Innovation in a Multiethnic Church*. Bloomington, IN: Indiana University Press.

———. 2008. "Fluid Ethnicity and Ethnic Transcendence in Multiracial Churches." *Journal for the Scientific Study of Religion* 47, no. 1: 11–16.

———. 2009. "Affinity, Identity, and Transcendence: The Experience of Religious Racial Integration in Diverse Congregations." *Journal for the Scientific Study of Religion* 48, no. 1: 53–68.

———. 2015. "Conceptual Pathways to Ethnic Transcendence in Diverse Churches: Theoretical Reflections on the Achievement of Successfully Integrated Congregations." *Religions* 6, no. 3: 1048–66.

Marti, Gerardo, and Gladys Ganiel. 2014. *The Deconstructed Church: Understanding Emerging Christianity*. New York: Oxford University Press.

Martinez, Brandon C. 2018. "The Integration of Racial and Ethnic Minorities into White Congregations." *Sociological Inquiry* 88, no. 3: 467–93.

Marx, Karl. 1978. "Contribution to the Critique of Hegel's Philosophy of Right: Introduction (1844)." In *The Marx-Engels Reader*, edited by R. C. Tucker, 53–65. New York: W. W. Norton & Company.

Massey, Douglas S., and Monica Espinoza Higgins. 2011. "The Effect of Immigration on Religious Belief and Practice: A Theologizing or Alienating Experience?" *Social Science Research* 40, no. 5: 1371–89.

Matthews, Todd L., John P. Bartkowski, and Tyrone Chase. 2016. "Race and Ethnicity." In *Handbook of Religion and Society*, edited by David Yamane, 421–41. Switzerland: Springer International Publishing.

Mattis, Jacqueline S., Kiu Eubanks, Alix A. Zapata, Nyasha Grayman, Max Belkin, N'Jeri K. Mitchell, and Sharon Cooper. 2004. "Factors Influencing Religious Non-Attendance among African American Men: A Multimethod Analysis." *Review of Religious Research* 45, no. 4: 386–403.

McCright, Aaron M., and Riley E. Dunlap. 2008. "The Nature and Social Bases of Progressive Social Movement Ideology: Examining Public Opinion toward Social Movements." *Sociological Quarterly* 49, no. 4: 825–48.

McDaniel, Eric. 2003. "Black Clergy in the 2000 Election." *Journal for the Scientific Study of Religion* 42, no. 4: 533–46.

McGuire, Meredith. 2008. *Lived Religion: Faith and Practice in Everyday Life*. New York: Oxford University Press.

McPherson, Miller, Lynn Smith-Lovin, and James M. Cook. 2001. "Birds of a Feather: Homophily in Social Networks." *Annual Review of Sociology* 27: 415–44.

Miller, Alan S., and John P. Hoffmann. 1995. "Risk and Religion: An Explanation of Gender Differences in Religiosity." *Journal for the Scientific Study of Religion* 34, no. 1: 63–75.

Min, Pyong Gap. 1992. "The Structure and Social Functions of Korean Immigrant Churches in the United States." *International Migration Review* 26, no. 4: 1370–94.

———. 2010. *Preserving Ethnicity Through Religion in America: Korean Protestants and Indian Hindus Across Generations*. New York: New York University Press.

Min, Pyong Gap, and Dae Young Kim. 2005. "Intergenerational Transmission of Religion and Culture: Korean Protestants in the U.S." *Sociology of Religion* 66, no. 3: 263–82.

Mooney, Margarita. 2009. *Faith Makes Us Live: Surviving and Thriving in the Haitian Diaspora*. Berkeley: University of California Press.

Morris, Aldon. 1984. *The Origins of the Civil Rights Movement: Black Communities Organizing for Change*. New York: Collier-Macmillan.

Morris, Alex. 2019. "The Generous Gospel of Mayor Pete." *Rolling Stone*, November 20, 2019. https://www.rollingstone.com/politics/politics-features/mayor-pete-buttigieg-faith-christianity-primary-election-913808/.

Mosher, William D., Linda B. Williams, and David P. Johnson. 1992. "Religion and Fertility in the United States: New Patterns." *Demography* 29, no. 2: 199–214.

Mouw, Ted. 2003. "Social Capital and Finding a Job: Do Contacts Matter?" *American Sociological Review* 68, no. 6: 868–98.

Mulder, Mark, Gerardo Marti, and Aida I. Ramos. 2017. *Latino Protestants in America: Growing and Diverse*. Lanham, MD: Rowman & Littlefield.

Mutchler, Jan E., Jeffrey A. Burr, and Francis G. Caro. 2003. "From Paid Worker to Volunteer: Leaving the Paid Workforce and Volunteering in Later Life." *Social Forces* 81, no. 4: 1267–93.

Nagel, Joane. 1997. *American Indian Ethnic Renewal: Red Power and the Resurgence of Identity and Culture.* New York: Oxford University Press.

Neitz, Mary Jo. 2014. "Becoming Visible: Religion and Gender in Sociology." *Sociology of Religion* 75, no. 4: 511–23.

Nelson, Timothy J. 2005. *Every Time I Feel the Spirit: Religious Experience and Ritual in an African American Church.* New York: New York University Press.

———. 2008. "At Ease with Our Own Kind: Worship Practices and Class Segregation in American Religion." In *Religion and Class in America: Culture, History, and Politics,* edited by Sean McCloud and William A. Mirola, 45–68. International Studies in Religion and Society, vol. 7. Leiden: Brill.

Nevin, David, and Robert E. Bills. 1976. *The Schools That Fear Built.* Washington, DC: Acropolis Books.

Noll, Mark A. 2009. "Religion and the American Founding." In *The Oxford Handbook of Religion and American Politics,* edited by Corwin E. Smidt, Lyman A. Kellstedt, and James Guth, 43–68. New York: Oxford University Press.

Nordin, Virginia Davis, and William Lloyd Turner. 1980. "More than Segregation Academies: The Growing Protestant Fundamentalist Schools." *Phi Delta Kappan* 61, no. 6: 391–94.

Norris, Pippa, and Ronald Inglehart. 2011. *Sacred and Secular: Religion and Politics Worldwide.* New York: Cambridge University Press.

Okihiro, Gary Y. 1984. "Religion and Resistance in America's Concentration Camps." *Phylon* 45, no. 3: 220–33.

Okuwobi, Oneya Fennell. 2019. "'Everything That I've Done Has Always Been Multiethnic': Biographical Work among Leaders of Multiracial Churches." *Sociology of Religion* 80, no. 4: 478–95.

Olson, Daniel V. A. 2019. "The Influence of Your Neighbors' Religions on You, Your Attitudes and Behaviors, and Your Community." *Sociology of Religion* 80, no. 2: 147–67.

Omi, Michael, and Howard Winant. 1986. *Racial Formation in the United States.* New York: Routledge.

Park, Jerry Z., and Samuel H. Reimer. 2002. "Revisiting the Social Sources of American Christianity 1972–1998." *Journal for the Scientific Study of Religion* 41, no. 4: 733–46.

Park, Jerry Z., and Kenneth Vaughan. 2018. "Sacred Ethnic Boundaries: Korean American Religions." In *A Companion to Korean American Studies,* edited by Rachael Miyung Joo and Shelley Sang-Hee Lee, 383–417. Brill's Companions to the Americas: History, Societies, Environments, and Cultures, vol. 1. Leiden: Brill.

Park, Kristin. 1998. "The Religious Construction of Sanctuary Provision in Two Congregations." *Sociological Spectrum* 18, no. 4: 393–421.

Pattillo-McCoy, Mary. 1998. "Church Culture as a Strategy of Action in the Black Community." *American Sociological Review* 63, no. 6: 767–84.

Pearce, Lisa D., and Melinda L. Denton. 2011. *A Faith of Their Own: Stability and Change in the Religiosity of America's Adolescents*. New York: Oxford University Press.

Pearce, Lisa D., and Arland Thornton. 2007. "Religious Identity and Family Ideologies in the Transition to Adulthood." *Journal of Marriage and Family* 69, no. 5: 1227–43.

Pearce, Lisa D., Jeremy E. Uecker, and Melinda Lundquist Denton. 2019. "Religion and Adolescent Outcomes: How and Under What Conditions Religion Matters." *Annual Review of Sociology* 45, no. 1: 201–22.

Perry, Samuel L. 2012. "Racial Habitus, Moral Conflict, and White Moral Hegemony within Interracial Evangelical Organizations." *Qualitative Sociology* 35, no. 1: 89–108.

———. 2013. "Multiracial Church Attendance and Support for Same-Sex Romantic and Family Relationships." *Sociological Inquiry* 83, no. 2: 259–85.

Pew Research Center. 2014. "The Shifting Religious Identity of Latinos in the United States." Pew Research Center. http://www.pewforum.org/2014/05/07/the-shifting-religious-identity-of-latinos-in-the-united-states/.

———. 2015. "America's Changing Religious Landscape." Pew Research Center. http://www.pewforum.org/2015/05/12/americas-changing-religious-landscape/.

———. 2016. "The Gender Gap in Religion around the World." Pew Research Center. http://assets.pewresearch.org/wp-content/uploads/sites/11/2016/03/Religion-and-Gender-Full-Report.pdf.

———. 2019. "Origins of the U.S. Immigrant Population, 1960–2016." Accessed February 2, 2019. http://www.pewhispanic.org/chart/immigrant-statistical-portrait-origins-of-the-u-s-immigrant-population/.

Polson, Edward C. 2016. "Putting Civic Participation in Context: Examining the Effects of Congregational Structure and Culture." *Review of Religious Research* 58, no. 1: 75–100.

Polson, Edward C., and Kevin D. Dougherty. 2018. "Worshiping across the Color Line: The Influence of Congregational Composition on Whites' Friendship Networks and Racial Attitudes." *Sociology of Race and Ethnicity*: 1–15.

Pratt, Tia Noelle. 2010. "Finding a Place at the Table: Identity Formation Among African-American Catholics." PhD diss., Fordham University, 2010. https://fordham.bepress.com/dissertations/AAI3431925.

Presser, Stanley, and Mark Chaves. 2007. "Is Religious Service Attendance Declining?" *Journal for the Scientific Study of Religion* 46, no. 3: 417–23.

Prothero, Stephen. 2016. *Why Liberals Win the Culture Wars (Even When They Lose Elections): The Battles That Define America from Jefferson's Heresies to Gay Marriage.* New York: HarperCollins.

Putnam, Robert D., and David E. Campbell. 2010. *American Grace: How Religion Divides and Unites Us.* Simon & Schuster.

Pyle, Ralph E., and James D. Davidson. 2014. "Social Reproduction and Religious Stratification." In *Religion and Inequality in America: Research and Theory on Religion's Role in Stratification,* edited by Lisa A. Keister and Darren E. Sherkat, 195–218. New York: Cambridge University Press.

"Race/Ethnicity and Religion in American History." n.d. Association of Religion Data Archives. Accessed January 20, 2019. http://www.thearda.com /learningcenter/modules/module42.asp.

Ramos, Aida I., Gerardo Martí, and Mark T. Mulder. 2018. "The Growth and Diversity of Latino Protestants in America." *Religion Compass* 12, no. 7: 1–11.

Read, Jen'nan Ghazal. 2003. "The Sources of Gender Role Attitudes among Christian and Muslim Arab-American Women." *Sociology of Religion* 64, no. 2: 207–22.

Rebhun, Uzi. 1995. "Geographic Mobility and Religioethnic Identification: Three Jewish Communities in the United States." *Journal for the Scientific Study of Religion* 34, no. 4: 485–98.

Reimers, David. 1998. *Unwelcome Strangers: American Identity and the Turn against Immigration.* New York: Columbia University Press.

"Religion in America: U.S. Religious Data, Demographics and Statistics." 2018. Washington, DC: Pew Research Center. http://www.pewforum.org/religious -landscape-study/.

Religion in Public. n.d. *Religion in Public.* Accessed January 20, 2020. https:// religioninpublic.blog/.

Roof, Wade. 1999. *Spiritual Marketplace: Baby Boomers and the Remaking of American Religion.* Princeton, NJ: Princeton University Press.

Roof, Wade, and William McKinney. 1987. *American Mainline Religion: Its Changing Shape and Future.* New Brunswick, NJ: Rutgers University Press.

Sawyer, Mary R. 2001. "Theocratic, Prophetic, and Ecumenical: Political Roles of African American Clergy." In *Christian Clergy in American Politics,* edited by Sue Crawford and Laura R. Olson, 66–84. Baltimore: Johns Hopkins University Press.

Scheitle, Christopher P., and Kevin D. Dougherty. 2010. "Race, Diversity, and Membership Duration in Religious Congregations." *Sociological Inquiry* 80, no. 3: 405–23.

Scheitle, Christopher P., Jennifer B. Kane, and Jennifer Van Hook. 2011. "Demographic Imperatives and Religious Markets: Considering the

Individual and Interactive Roles of Fertility and Switching in Group Growth." *Journal for the Scientific Study of Religion* 50, no. 3: 470–82.

Schleifer, Cyrus, and Mark Chaves. 2014. "Family Formation and Religious Service Attendance: Untangling Marital and Parental Effects." *Sociological Methods & Research* 46, no. 1:125–52.

Schnabel, Landon. 2015. "How Religious Are American Women and Men? Gender Differences and Similarities." *Journal for the Scientific Study of Religion* 54, no. 3: 616–22.

———. 2016a. "Gender and Homosexuality Attitudes across Religious Groups from the 1970s to 2014: Similarity, Distinction, and Adaptation." *Social Science Research* 55: 31–47.

———. 2016b. "The Gender Pray Gap: Wage Labor and the Religiosity of High-Earning Women and Men." *Gender & Society* 30, no. 4: 643–69.

Schnabel, Landon, and Sean Bock. 2017. "The Persistent and Exceptional Intensity of American Religion: A Response to Recent Research." *Sociological Science* 4: 686–700.

Schwadel, Philip. 2010. "Period and Cohort Effects on Religious Nonaffiliation and Religious Disaffiliation: A Research Note." *Journal for the Scientific Study of Religion* 49, no. 2: 311–19.

———. 2011a. "Age, Period, and Cohort Effects on U.S. Religious Service Attendance: The Declining Impact of Sex, Southern Residence, and Catholic Affiliation." *Sociology of Religion* 71, no. 1: 2–24.

———. 2011b. "Age, Period, and Cohort Effects on Religious Activities and Beliefs." *Social Science Research* 40, no. 1: 181–92.

———. 2014. "Birth Cohort Changes in the Association Between College Education and Religious Non-Affiliation." *Social Forces* 93, no. 2: 719–46.

———. 2015. "Explaining Cross-National Variation in the Effect of Higher Education on Religiosity." *Journal for the Scientific Study of Religion* 54, no. 2: 402–18.

———. 2016. "Social Class." In *Handbook of Religion and Society*, edited by David Yamane, 345–72. Switzerland: Springer International Publishing.

Selby, Gary S. 2002. "Mocking the Sacred: Frederick Douglass's 'Slaveholder's Sermon' and the Antebellum Debate over Religion and Slavery." *Quarterly Journal of Speech* 88, no. 3: 326–41.

Shelton, Jason, and Michael O. Emerson. 2012. *Blacks and Whites in Christian America: How Racial Discrimination Shapes Religious Convictions*. New York: New York University Press.

Sherkat, Darren E. 2002. "Sexuality and Religious Commitment in the United States: An Empirical Examination." *Journal for the Scientific Study of Religion* 41, no. 2: 313–23.

———. 2008. "Beyond Belief: Atheism, Agnosticism, and Theistic Certainty in the United States." *Sociological Spectrum* 28, no. 5: 438–59.

———. 2014. *Changing Faith: The Dynamics and Consequences of Americans' Shifting Religious Identities*. New York: New York University Press.

Sherkat, Darren E., and Alfred Darnell. 1999. "The Effect of Parents' Fundamentalism on Children's Educational Attainment: Examining Differences by Gender and Children's Fundamentalism." *Journal for the Scientific Study of Religion* 38, no. 1: 23–35.

Skirbekk, Vegard, Eric Kaufmann, and Anne Goujon. 2010. "Secularism, Fundamentalism, or Catholicism? The Religious Composition of the United States to 2043." *Journal for the Scientific Study of Religion* 49, no. 2: 293–310.

Smith, Christian. 1996. *Disruptive Religion: The Force of Faith in Social-Movement Activism*. New York: Routledge.

———. 2017. *Religion: What It Is, How It Works, and Why It Matters*. Princeton, NJ: Princeton University Press.

Smith, Christian, and Michael Emerson. 1998. *American Evangelicalism: Embattled and Thriving*. Chicago: University of Chicago Press.

Smith, Christian, and Robert Faris. 2005. "Socioeconomic Inequality in the American Religious System: An Update and Assessment." *Journal for the Scientific Study of Religion* 44, no. 1: 95–104.

Smith, Christian, Brandon Vaidyanathan, Nancy Tatom Ammerman, José Casanova, Hilary Davidson, Elaine Howard Ecklund, John H. Evans, Philip S. Gorski, Mary Ellen Konieczny, Jason A. Springs, Jenny Trinitapoli, and Meredith Whitnah. 2013. "Roundtable on the Sociology of Religion: Twenty-Three Theses on the Status of Religion in American Sociology—A Mellon Working-Group Reflection." *Journal of the American Academy of Religion* 81, no. 4: 903–38.

Smith, Greg, and Linda Woodhead. 2018. "Religion and Brexit: Populism and the Church of England." *Religion, State and Society* 46, no. 3: 206–23.

Smith, Timothy L. 1978. "Religion and Ethnicity in America." *American Historical Review* 83, no. 5: 1155–85.

Smith, Tom W. 2007. "An Evaluation of Spanish Questions on the 2006 General Social Survey." GSS Methodological Report No. 109. Chicago: NORC.

Smith, Tom W., Peter Marsden, and Michael Hout. 2015. "General Social Surveys, 1972–2014 [Machine-Readable Data File] /Principal Investigator, Smith, Tom W.; Co-Principal Investigators, Peter V. Marsden and Michael Hout." Chicago: NORC.

Sokol, Jason. 2006. *There Goes My Everything: White Southerners in the Age of Civil Rights, 1945–1975*. New York: Alfred A. Knopf.

Stark, Rodney. 2002. "Physiology and Faith: Addressing the 'Universal' Gender Difference in Religious Commitment." *Journal for the Scientific Study of Religion* 41, no. 3: 495–507.

Stark, Rodney, and Roger Finke. 2000. *Acts of Faith: Explaining the Human Side of Religion*. Berkeley: University of California Press.

Stewart, Evan, Penny Edgell, and Jack Delehanty. 2018. "The Politics of Religious Prejudice and Tolerance for Cultural Others." *Sociological Quarterly* 59, no. 1: 17–39.

Stoltz Chinchilla, Norma, Nora Hamilton, and James Loucky. 2009. "The Sanctuary Movement and Central American Activism in Los Angeles." *Latin American Perspectives* 36, no. 6: 101–26.

Stolzenberg, Ross M., Mary Blair-Loy, and Linda J. Waite. 1995. "Religious Participation in Early Adulthood: Age and Family Life Cycle Effects on Church Membership." *American Sociological Review* 60, no. 1: 84–103.

Storm, Ingrid. 2018. "When Does Religiosity Matter for Attitudes to Immigration? The Impact of Economic Insecurity and Religious Norms in Europe." *European Societies* 20, no. 4: 595–620.

Stroope, Samuel. 2011. "How Culture Shapes Community: Bible Belief, Theological Unity, and a Sense of Belonging in Religious Congregations." *Sociological Quarterly* 52, no. 4: 568–92.

Stroope, Samuel, and Joseph O. Baker. 2014. "Structural and Cultural Sources of Community in American Congregations." *Social Science Research* 45: 1–17.

Suh, Sharon. 2004. *Being Buddhist in a Christian World: Gender and Community in a Korean American Temple.* Seattle: University of Washington Press.

Sullins, D. Paul. 2006. "Gender and Religion: Deconstructing Universality, Constructing Complexity." *American Journal of Sociology* 112, no. 3: 838–80.

Sullivan, Susan. 2011. *Living Faith: Everyday Religion and Mothers in Poverty.* Chicago: University of Chicago Press.

Sumerau, J. E. 2017. "'Some of Us Are Good, God-Fearing Folks': Justifying Religious Participation in an LGBT Christian Church." *Journal of Contemporary Ethnography* 46, no. 1: 3–29.

Sumerau, J. E., Ryan T. Cragun, and Lain A. B. Mathers. 2016a. "'I Found God in The Glory Hole': The Moral Career of a Gay Christian." *Sociological Inquiry* 86, no. 4: 618–40.

———. 2016b. "Contemporary Religion and the Cisgendering of Reality." *Social Currents* 3, no. 3: 293–311.

Suro, Roberto, Gabriel Escobar, Gretchen Livingston, Shirin Hakimzadeh, Luis Lugo, Sandra Stencel, and S. Chaudhry. 2007. "Changing Faiths: Latinos and the Transformation of American Religion." Pew Research Center. https:// www.pewresearch.org/wp-content/uploads/sites/7/2007/04/hispanics -religion-07-final-mar08.pdf

Suziedelis, Antanas, and Raymond H. Potvin. 1981. "Sex Differences in Factors Affecting Religiousness among Catholic Adolescents." *Journal for the Scientific Study of Religion* 20, no. 1: 38–51.

Swarts, Heidi. 2011. "Drawing New Symbolic Boundaries over Old Social Boundaries: Forging Social Movement Unity in Congregation-Based Community Organizing." *Sociological Perspectives* 54, no. 3: 453–77.

Taylor, Robert Joseph, Linda M. Chatters, Rukmalie Jayakody, and Jeffrey S. Levin. 1996. "Black and White Differences in Religious Participation: A Multisample Comparison." *Journal for the Scientific Study of Religion* 35, no. 4: 403–10.

Tepe, Sultan. 2013. "The Perils of Polarization and Religious Parties: The Democratic Challenges of Political Fragmentation in Israel and Turkey." *Democratization* 20, no. 5: 831–56.

Thornton, Arland. 2005. *Reading History Sideways: The Fallacy and Enduring Impact of the Developmental Paradigm on Family Life.* Chicago: University of Chicago Press.

Thumma, Scott L., and Warren Bird. 2015. "Megafaith for the Megacity: The Global Megachurch Phenomenon." In *The Changing World Religion Map*, edited by Stanley D. Brunn, 2331–52. Dordrecht: Springer International Publishing.

Thumma, Scott L., and Dave Travis. 2007. *Beyond Megachurch Myths: What We Can Learn from America's Largest Churches.* San Francisco, CA: Jossey-Bass.

Tranby, Eric, and Samantha E. Zulkowski. 2012. "Religion as Cultural Power: The Role of Religion in Influencing Americans' Symbolic Boundaries around Gender and Sexuality." *Sociology Compass* 6, no. 11: 870–82.

Tripp, Jason. 2014. "The Most Segregated Hour in America - Martin Luther King Jr." April 17, 1960. *YouTube* video 0:52. Accessed January 20, 2020. https://www.youtube.com/watch?v=1q881g1L_d8.

Tsitsos, William. 2003. "Race Differences in Congregational Social Service Activity." *Journal for the Scientific Study of Religion* 42, no. 2: 205–15.

Twenge, Jean M., Ryne A. Sherman, Julie J. Exline, and Joshua B. Grubbs. 2016. "Declines in American Adults' Religious Participation and Beliefs, 1972–2014." *SAGE Open* 6, no. 1. https://doi.org/10.1177%2F2158244016638133.

Uecker, Jeremy E. 2014. "Religion and Early Marriage in the United States: Evidence from the Add Health Study." *Journal for the Scientific Study of Religion* 53, no. 2: 392–415.

Uecker, Jeremy E., and Glenn Lucke. 2011. "Protestant Clergy and the Culture Wars: An Empirical Test of Hunter's Thesis." *Journal for the Scientific Study of Religion* 50, no. 4: 692–706.

Uecker, Jeremy E., and Lisa D. Pearce. 2017. "Conservative Protestantism and Horizontal Stratification in Education: The Case of College Selectivity." *Social Forces* 96, no. 2: 661–90.

Uecker, Jeremy E., Mark D. Regnerus, and Margaret L. Vaaler. 2007. "Losing My Religion: The Social Sources of Religious Decline in Early Adulthood." *Social Forces* 85, no. 4: 1667–92.

Uecker, Jeremy E., and Charles E. Stokes. 2008. "Early Marriage in the United States." *Journal of Marriage and Family* 70, no. 4: 835–46.

US Census Bureau. 2017a. "Educational Attainment in the United States: 2016." https://www.census.gov/data/tables/2016/demo/education-attainment/cps -detailed-tables.html.

———. 2017b. "2013-2017 Amercian Community Survey 5-Year Estimates." *American Fact Finder, United States Census Bureau.*

———. 2019. "U.S. Census Bureau QuickFacts: United States." https://www .census.gov/quickfacts/fact/table/US/PST045218#qf-headnote-a.

"U.S. Congregational Memberships: Maps." n.d. Association of Religion Data Archives. Accessed January 20, 2020. http://www.thearda.com /mapsReports/maps/Ardamap.asp?mo1=2001&alpha=&GRP2=1&map2=1.

Voas, David, and Mark Chaves. 2016a. "Is the United States a Counterexample to the Secularization Thesis?" *American Journal of Sociology* 121, no. 5: 1517–56.

———. 2018. "Even Intense Religiosity is Declining in the United States." *Sociological Science* 5: 694-710.

Voas, David, and Alasdair Crockett. 2005. "Religion in Britain: Neither Believing nor Belonging." *Sociology: The Journal of the British Sociological Association* 39, no. 1: 11–28.

Voas, David, Siobhan McAndrew, and Ingrid Storm. 2013. "Modernization and the Gender Gap in Religiosity: Evidence from Cross-National European Surveys." *KZfSS Kölner Zeitschrift für Soziologie und Sozialpsychologie* 65, no. 1: 259–83.

Voas, David, Daniel Olson V. A., and Alasdair Crockett. 2002. "Religious Pluralism and Participation: Why Previous Research Is Wrong." *American Sociological Review* 67, no. 2: 212–30.

Wachholtz, Amy B., and Usha Sambamoorthi. 2011. "National Trends in Prayer Use as a Coping Mechanism for Health Concerns: Changes from 2002 to 2007." *Psychology of Religion and Spirituality* 3, no. 2: 67–77.

Wachholtz, Amy B., and Usha Sambamthoori. 2013. "National Trends in Prayer Use as a Coping Mechanism for Depression: Changes from 2002 to 2007." *Journal of Religion and Health* 52, no. 4: 1356–68.

Wald, Kenneth, and Allison Calhoun-Brown. 2014. *Religion and Politics in the United States.* 7th ed. Lanham, MD: Rowman & Littlefield.

Walter, Tony, and Grace Davie. 1998. "The Religiosity of Women in the Modern West." *British Journal of Sociology* 49, no. 4: 640–60.

Warner, R. Stephen. 1993. "Work in Progress Toward a New Paradigm for the Sociological Study of Religion in the United States." *American Journal of Sociology* 98, no. 5: 1044–93.

Whitehead, Andrew L. 2017. "Institutionalized Norms, Practical Organizational Activity, and Loose Coupling: Inclusive Congregations' Responses to Homosexuality." *Journal for the Scientific Study of Religion* 56, no. 4: 820–35.

Whitehead, Andrew L., Samuel L. Perry, and Joseph O. Baker. 2018. "Make America Christian Again: Christian Nationalism and Voting for Donald Trump in the 2016 Presidential Election." *Sociology of Religion* 79, no. 2: 147–71.

Whitehead, Andrew L., Landon Schnabel, and Samuel L. Perry. 2018. "Gun Control in the Crosshairs: Christian Nationalism and Opposition to Stricter Gun Laws." *Socius* 4: 1–13.

Wilcox, W. Bradford, Mark Chaves, and David Franz. 2004. "Focused on the Family? Religious Traditions, Family Discourse, and Pastoral Practice." *Journal for the Scientific Study of Religion* 43, no. 4: 491–504.

Wilcox, W. Bradford, Andrew J. Cherlin, Jeremy E. Uecker, and Matthew Messel. 2012. "No Money, No Honey, No Church: The Deinstitutionalization of Religious Life among the White Working Class." In *Religion, Work, and Inequality*, edited by Lisa A. Keister, John McCarthy, and Roger Finke, 227–51. Research in the Sociology of Work, vol. 23. Bingley: Emerald Group Publishing Limited.

Wilde, Melissa J. 2018a. "Editorial: 'Complex Religion: Intersections of Religion and Inequality.'" *Social Inclusion* 6, no. 2: 83–86.

———. 2018b. "Complex Religion: Interrogating Assumptions of Independence in the Study of Religion." *Sociology of Religion* 79, no. 3: 287–98.

———. Wilde, Melissa J. 2019. *Birth Control Battles: How Race and Class Divided American Religion*. Berkeley: University of California Press.

Wilde, Melissa J., and Sabrina Danielsen. 2014. "Fewer and Better Children: Race, Class, Religion, and Birth Control Reform in America." *American Journal of Sociology* 119, no. 6: 1710–60.

Wilde, Melissa J., and Patricia Tevington. 2015. "Complex Religion: Toward a Better Understanding of the Ways in Which Religion Intersects with Inequality." In *Emerging Trends in the Social and Behavioral Sciences*, edited by Robert Scott and Marlis Buchmann, with Stephen Kossyln, 1–13. Hoboken, NJ: John Wiley & Sons, Inc.

Winstead, Kevin. 2017. "'Authentically Black, and Truly Catholic': A Survey of the Study on Black Catholics." *Sociology Compass* 11, no. 10: e12517.

Wood, Richard L., and Brad R. Fulton. 2015. *A Shared Future: Faith-Based Organizing for Racial Equity and Ethical Democracy*. Chicago: University of Chicago Press.

Woodhead, Linda. 2008. "Gendering Secularization Theory." *Social Compass* 55, no. 2: 187–93.

Wright, Bradley R. E., Michael Wallace, Annie Scola Wisnesky, Christopher M. Donnelly, Stacy Missari, and Christine Zozula. 2015. "Religion, Race, and Discrimination: A Field Experiment of How American Churches Welcome Newcomers." *Journal for the Scientific Study of Religion* 54, no. 2: 185–204.

Wuthnow, Robert. 1988. *The Restructuring of American Religion: Society and Faith since World War II*. Princeton, NJ: Princeton University Press.

———. 1998. *After Heaven: Spirituality in America since the 1950s*. Berkeley: University of California Press.

———. 2007. *After the Baby Boomers: How Twenty- and Thirty-Somethings Are Shaping the Future of American Religion*. Princeton, NJ: Princeton University Press.

———. 2015. *Inventing American Religion: Polls, Surveys, and The Tenuous Quest for a Nation's Faith*. New York: Oxford University Press.

Wuthnow, Robert, and Kevin Christiano. 1979. "The Effects of Residential Migration on Church Attendance in the United States." In *The Religious Dimension: New Directions in Quantitative Research*, edited by Robert Wuthnow, 257–76. New York: Academic Press.

Yancey, George. 1999. "An Examination of the Effects of Residential and Church Integration on Racial Attitudes of Whites." *Sociological Perspectives* 42, no. 2: 279–304.

———. 2005. "A Comparison of Religiosity between European-Americans, African-Americans, Hispanic-Americans and Asian-Americans." *Research in the Social Scientific Study of Religion* 16: 83.

Yancey, George, and Michael O. Emerson. 2003. "Integrated Sundays: An Exploratory Study into the Formation of Multiracial Churches." *Sociological Focus* 36, no. 2: 111–26.

Yancey, George, and Ye Jung Kim. 2008. "Racial Diversity, Gender Equality, and SES Diversity in Christian Congregations: Exploring the Connections of Racism, Sexism, and Classism in Multiracial and Nonmultiracial Churches." *Journal for the Scientific Study of Religion* 47, no. 1: 103–11.

Yang, Fenggang. 2002. "Religious Diversity Among the Chinese in America." In *Religions in Asian America: Building Faith Communities*, edited by Pyong Gap Min and Jung Ha Kim, 71–98. Walnut Creek, CA: AltaMira Press.

Yang, Fenggang, and Helen Rose Ebaugh. 2001. "Transformations in New Immigrant Religions and Their Global Implications." *American Sociological Review* 66, no. 2: 269–88.

Yang, Yang, and Kenneth C. Land. 2016. *Age-Period-Cohort Analysis: New Models, Methods, and Empirical Applications*. Boca Raton, FL: CRC Press.

Yinger, John M. 1970. *The Scientific Study of Religion*. London: Macmillan.

Yoo, David. 2002. "A Religious History of Japanese Americans in California." In *Religions in Asian America: Building Faith Communities*, edited by Jung Kim and Pyong Gap Min, 121–42. Walnut Creek, CA: AltaMira Press.

"Young Men, Young Men, and Religion: How Young Adult Religiosity Differs by Gender." n.d. Association of Religion Data Archives, Accessed January 20, 2020. http://www.thearda.com/learningcenter/modules/module23.asp.

Young, Michael P. 2002. "Confessional Protest: The Religious Birth of U.S. National Social Movements." *American Sociological Review* 67, no. 5: 660–88.

Yukich, Grace. 2013a. *One Family under God: Immigration Politics and Progressive Religion in America*. New York: Oxford University Press.

———. 2013b. "Constructing the Model Immigrant: Movement Strategy and Immigrant Deservingness in the New Sanctuary Movement." *Social Problems* 60, no. 3: 302–20.

Yukich, Grace, and Ruth Braunstein. 2014. "Encounters at the Religious Edge: Variation in Religious Expression Across Interfaith Advocacy and Social Movement Settings." *Journal for the Scientific Study of Religion* 53, no. 4: 791–807.

Zhai, Jiexia Elisa, and Charles E. Stokes. 2009. "Ethnic, Family, and Social Contextual Influences on Asian American Adolescents' Religiosity." *Sociological Spectrum* 29, no. 2: 201–26.

Zhang, Gehui, and Heying Jenny Zhan. 2009. "Beyond the Bible and the Cross: A Social and Cultural Analysis of Chinese Elders' Participation in Christian Congregations in the United States." *Sociological Spectrum* 29, no. 2: 295–317.

Zubaida, Sami. 2000. "Trajectories of Political Islam: Egypt, Iran and Turkey." *Political Quarterly* 71, no. 1: 60–78.

Zuberi, Tukufu. 2001. *Thicker Than Blood: How Racial Statistics Lie*. Minneapolis, MN: University of Minnesota Press.

Zuckerman, Phil. 2002. "The Sociology of Religion of W. E. B. Du Bois." *Sociology of Religion* 63, no. 2: 239–53.

Index

abortion, 118–22, 119*fig*

adolescents, 45; demographic trends over time, 70–75, 72*fig*; life cycle changes in religiousness, 58–60

African Americans: Black-White religious differences, 21–23; demographic perspective on religion, 12–15, 126–30; diversity within congregations, 91–95, 92*fig*, 130–32; explanations for religious differences, 31–35; megachurches and, 89; racialization of religion, 35–36; religion and racial hierarchies, 114–18; religious trends, race, gender, and education, 48–55, 50*fig*, 52*fig*, 53*fig*; socioeconomic class and, 41–42; trends in religiousness over time, 27–29, 28*fig*, 29*fig*; use of term, 20; worship styles, 32–33. *See also* Black Protestantism

afterlife, belief in, 47, 67

age: effect on religiousness, 12–13, 45*box*; gender and religiousness, 45; life cycle changes, 58–60

age effects, 56; demographic trends, 126, 129–30; GSS data analysis, 63–67, 64*tab*; impact of, 58–60; residential mobility and, 69–70. *See also* cohort effects

Aggregate Religiosity Index (ARI), 10–11, 10*fig*

Arab Americans: definition of, 26; demographic perspective on religion, 12–15; religious patterns, 25–26

Asian Americans: demographic perspective on religion, 12–15; diversity within congregations, 91–95, 92*fig*; immigration, history of, 110–14, 112*fig*; migration experience, effect on religiousness, 33–35; religious patterns, 23–25; use of term, 20

Association of Religion Data Archives (ARDA), 18, 35*box*, 85

Australia, general trends in religion, 9

Baby Boomer Generation, 62

Baptists: affiliation data, 7; political efforts by, 107, 115, 121; socioeconomic class and, 39–40, 40*fig*

Bellah, Robert, 4

Berger, Peter, 4

Bible: Black-White religious differences, 21–23; as literal document, 9, 39, 63; use in education system, 109

birth control, 109

birth rates, 67–70, 79–82

Black Protestantism: building blocks of, 32; demographic trends over time, 70–75, 72*fig*; diversity within congregations, 94–95, 130–32; gender and religiousness,

Black Protestantism (*continued*)
47; religion and racial hierarchies, 115–18; as semi-involuntary institution, 33. *See also* Black population

Blue laws, 108–9, 151n31

Bob Jones University (BJU), 117

boundary-making processes: 2016 presidential election, 102–3; drawing and defending boundaries, 106, 122–24; Protestant dominance, history of US and, 106–10; religion and racial hierarchies, 114–18; religious affiliation, overview of, 102–6, 104*fig*; sex and gender morality wars, 118–22, 119*fig*

Brown v. Board of Education of Topeka (1954), 117

Buddhists: Asian American religious patterns, 24–25; demographic trends over time, 72*fig*, 73–74; general trends in religion, 7–11, 8*fig*, 10*fig*; immigration policy and, 111–12; Japanese Americans, discrimination against, 109–10; political representation by, 31; socioeconomic class and, 41

Buttigieg, Pete, 105

California: abortion laws, 121; Proposition 187, 113

Campbell, David, 57

Canada: general trends in religion, 9, 63; immigrants from, 112, 112*fig*

Catholics: 2016 presidential election and, 102–3; Black-White religious differences, 21–22; conversion to other faiths, 29, 30*fig*; demographic trends over time, 70–75, 72*fig*; diversity within congregations, 94–95; general trends in religion, 7–11, 8*fig*, 10*fig*; immigration, US history of, 108–9, 113; Latinx trends over time, 29–31, 30*fig*; socioeconomic class and, 40, 40*fig*, 41–42

Central America: immigrant religious affiliation, 23; immigration from, 20; undocumented immigrants, 114

Chaves, Mark, 84

Chinese Americans: migration experience, effect on religiousness, 34; religious patterns, 23–25. *See also* Asian American population

Christianity: Arab American religious patterns, 26; Asian American religious patterns, 24–25; demographic trends over time, 70–75, 72*fig*; gender and religiousness, 44–45; megachurches, 88–90;

political dominance in US history, 106–10. *See also* Black Protestantism; Catholics; Evangelical Protestants; mainline Protestants; Protestants

Christian nationalism, 17, 118, 121–24, 132

Christian Voice, 58

church attendance: *See* religious service attendance

Church World Service, 111

Civil Rights Act (1964), 116

Civil Rights Movement, 115–18

class. *See* socioeconomic class

clergy: Black clergy, 91; Civil Rights Movement participation, 115–16; congregation trends and, 16, 100; diversity of, 91, 131; female clergy members, 91, 131; in immigrant communities, 34; multiracial congregations, 96, 99; social and political activism by, 116, 119–20, 133 (*See also* politics)

cohort, defined, 60–61

cohort effects, 56, 60–67, 64*tab*, 129–30. *See also* age effects

cohort replacement, 63, 64*tab*, 65

congregations: average size of, 86; changes over time, 15–16; diversity in congregation types, 90–91, 131–32; diversity in members of, 91–95, 92*fig*; diversity within, explanations and implications, 95–101, 130–32; megachurches, overview of, 88–90; multisite churches, 87; National Congregations Study (NCS), 84–86; number of, 84; resources and cost concerns, 87–88; stability of, 84; trends, future challenges, 130–32; trends, history, and characteristics, 86–88; types of, 83

conservative Christians: Chinese immigrant conversion to, 24, 33; female clergy and, 99; general trends in religion, 3, 5, 7–11, 8*fig*, 10*fig*; political and social activism, 57–58, 62; socioeconomic status and, 39, 42; worship styles, 22. *See also* Evangelical Protestants; politics

Coons, Chris, 105

data sources, overview of, 5–6; age effects and, 59–60; congregational surveys, limitations of, 84–85

death rates, 67–70

de facto congregationalism, 34

demographics: age effects, 56–60, 63–67, 64*tab*; cohort effects, 56–57, 60–67, 64*tab*; internal migration (mobility),

69–70; period effects, 56–58, 63–67, 64*tab*; perspective on change in American religion, 11–15; prayer, trends over time, 78–79, 79*tab*; predicting future trends, 79–82; religious affiliation trends, 70–75, 72*fig*; religious service attendance, 75–78, 77*tab*; shifting demographic composition, 67–70; trends, overview of, 126–30

Denmark, trends in religion, 8

dimensions of religiousness, 3

Displaced Persons Act (1948), 111

diversity, in congregations, 16, 91–101, 92*fig*, 130–32. *See also* ethnicity; gender; race

Du Bois, W.E.B., 35–36

Durkheim, Émile, 4

East Indian Americans, religious patterns, 23–25

education level: Black Protestants, 30–31; Chinese Americans, 24; cohort effects and, 62–63; demographic perspective on religion, 14, 126–30; demographic trends over time, 70–75, 72*fig*; religious affiliation and, 39–40, 40*fig*; religious trends, race, gender, and education, 48–55, 50*fig*, 52*fig*, 53*fig*. *See also* socioeconomic class

education system: desegregation and integration, 115–17; public *vs.* private, 109, 117–18

Ellis, Rachel, 48–49

El Salvador, immigrants from, 20

Emerging Church Movement (ECM), 131–32

Episcopalians, socioeconomic class and, 39–40, 40*fig*

ethnicity: Arab American religious patterns, 25–26; Asian American religious patterns, 23–25; Association of Religion Data Archives (ARDA), 35*box*; Black-White religious differences, 21–23; demographic perspective on religion, 12–15, 126–30; demographic trends over time, 70–75, 72*fig*; diversity trends within congregations, 91–95, 92*fig*, 130–32; diversity within congregations, explanations and implications, 95–101; explanations for religious differences, 31–35; Latinx religious patterns, 23; migration rates, 68–70; prayer, trends over time, 78–79, 79*tab*; predicting future trends, 79–82; racial/ethnic groups, use of term, 20; racialization of religion, 35–36; service attendance, trends over time, 76–77, 77*tab*; socioeconomic class and, 41–42; trends in religiousness over time, 26–29, 28*fig*, 29*fig*

ethnic transcendence, 96–97

European immigration, US history of, 108–9

Evangelical Protestants: 2016 presidential election and, 102–3; anti-Muslim sentiment, 113; conservative political movement and, 57–58; demographic trends over time, 70–75, 72*fig*; diversity within congregations, 94–95; general trends in religion, 7–11, 8*fig*, 10*fig*; Korean migration experience, effect on religiousness, 34–35; Latinx religious patterns, 23, 29–31, 30*fig*; megachurches, 89–90; private education and race, 117–18; sex and gender morality wars, 118–22, 119*fig*; socioeconomic class and, 40, 40*fig*. *See also* Pentecostals; Southern Baptists

Falwell, Jerry, 107, 121

family formation: demographic perspective on religion, 14, 80–81, 134; socioeconomic class and, 43; women's roles and, 47–48, 61, 128

"family values," 118, 121–24

fertility rates, 67–70, 109

Filipino Americans, religious patterns, 23–25

France, trends in religion, 8

Geertz, Clifford, 4

gender: clergy trends, 99; cultural expectations, 48–49; demographic perspective on religion, 13–14, 70–75, 72*fig*, 126–30; female clergy, 91, 99, 131; personal identity and, 38; political morality wars, 118–22, 119*fig*; prayer, trends over time, 78–79, 79*tab*; religiousness and, 44–48, 46*fig*; religious trends, race, gender, and education, 48–55, 50*fig*, 52*fig*, 53*fig*; service attendance, demographics of, 75–78, 77*tab*. *See also* men; women

General Social Survey (GSS), 5–6, 10–11, 10*fig*; data limitations, 27; gender equality attitudes, 118; not affiliated, trends over time, 63–67, 64*tab*, 137–38n11; prayer, trends over time, 78–79, 79*tab*; racial/ethnic trends, 27–31, 28*fig*, 29*fig*, 30*fig*; religious affiliation, trends over time, 71–75, 72*fig*; service attendance, trends over time, 75–78, 77*tab*

generational comparisons, 60–67, 64*tab*. *See also* cohort effects

God, belief in, 5, 9

Graham, Billy, 115

Great Britain, trends in religion, 8

Great Depression, 60–61
Guatemalan immigrants, 20

Hart-Cellar Immigration Act (1965), 111–12
Hindus: Asian American religious patterns,
    24–25; demographic trends over time,
    72*fig*, 73–74; general trends in religion,
    7–11, 8*fig*, 10*fig*; immigration policy and,
    111–12; migration experience, effect on
    religiousness, 33; socioeconomic class
    and, 41
historical perspective: colonial and early
    American experience, 106–8; drawing
    and defending boundaries, 106, 122–24;
    overview of, 16–17; Protestant dominance,
    history of US and, 106–10; religion and
    racial hierarchies, 114–18; religious affilia-
    tion, overview of, 102–6, 104*fig*; sex and
    gender morality wars, 118–22, 119*fig*; US
    immigration history, 108–14, 112*fig*
homophily, 95
homosexuality, 119. *See also* LGBTQ+ popula-
    tion; sexuality

immigration: Asian immigration trends,
    24–25; current debates about, 132–33;
    demographic trends over time, 70–75,
    72*fig*; diversity within congregations,
    94–95, 131; migration experience, effect
    on religious behavior, 33–35; migration
    rates, 68–70; post–World War II, 110–14,
    112*fig*; predicting future trends, 79–82;
    quotas for, 111; racialization of religion,
    35–36; service attendance, trends over
    time, 77, 77*tab*; trends in, 19–20; US
    history of prejudice toward, 108–10
Immigration Act (1965), 112
"In God We Trust," 1–2
intentional living communities, 131–32
internal migration, 69–70
Ireland, trends in religion, 8
Islam. *See* Muslims
Israel, 26
Italy, trends in religion, 8

Japanese Americans: discrimination against,
    109–10; migration experience, effect on
    religiousness, 34–35. *See also* Asian
    American population
Jewish population: demographic trends over
    time, 70–75, 72*fig*; gender and religious-
    ness, 44–45; general trends in religion,
    7–11, 8*fig*, 10*fig*; immigration, US history

of, 111, 113; socioeconomic class and,
    39–40, 40*fig*
Jim Crow laws, 115

King Jr., Rev. Martin Luther, 35–36, 116
Korean Americans: migration experience,
    effect on religiousness, 34–35; religious
    patterns, 23–25. *See also* Asian American
    population

labor force participation, 128, 129; demo-
    graphic shift and, 70; demographic trends
    over time, 70–75, 72*fig*; gender and, 48.
    See also occupation
Latinx American population: in congrega-
    tions, 91; demographic perspective on
    religion, 12–15; diversity within congrega-
    tions, 91–95, 92*fig*, 130–32; immigration,
    US history of, 111–14, 112*fig*; religious
    trends in, 23; socioeconomic class and,
    41–42; trends in religiousness over time,
    29–31, 30*fig*; use of term, 20
Latter-day Saints (LDS) (Mormon) Church, 7,
    8*tab*, 107–8
Latterell, Justin, 1
Lebanon, 26
LGBTQ+ population: diversity in congrega-
    tions, 99–100; lack of data for, 55; sex and
    gender morality wars, 118–22, 119*fig*.
    See also sexuality
life after death, belief in, 9
life cycle change, religiousness, 58–60, 63–67,
    64*tab*
Lincoln, Abraham, 1–2
"lived religion," 127–28

mainline Protestants: civil rights movement,
    116; congregation size, 91; definition of, 7;
    future predictions, 81; gender trends 47;
    Latinx population 23; racial diversity, 94;
    socioeconomic status 39; trends over
    time, 7, 8*tab*, 71, 72*figs*, 75; See also Epis-
    copalians; Presbyterians, Protestants
Marx, Karl, 4, 42
megachurches, 16, 85; congregation size,
    trends in, 86–88, 131; overview of, 88–90;
    types of, 89
men: demographic perspective on religion,
    70–75, 72*fig*, 126–30; Korean immigrants
    and role of men, 25; prayer, trends over
    time, 78–79, 79*tab*; religiousness meas-
    ures and, 44–48, 46*fig*, 127; religious
    trends, race, gender, and education,

48–55, 50*fig*, 52*fig*, 53*fig*, 127, 128, 129, 130; service attendance, demographics of, 45–48, 46*fig*, 75–78, 77*tab*, 134

migration, internal, 69–70

migration rates, 67–70

missionary work, 107

mobility, 69–70

money, "In God We Trust" on, 1–2

Moral Majority, 58

Mormon (Latter-day Saints (LDS)) church, 7, 8*tab*, 107–8

multiracial congregations, 92*fig*, 93–101, 130–32

multisite churches, 87

music, 32–33, 89

Muslims: Arab American religious patterns, 25–26; Black non-Latinx population, 31; congregations of, 91; demographic trends over time, 72*fig*, 73–74; gender and religiousness, 44–45; general trends in religion, 7–11, 8*fig*, 10*fig*; immigration policy and, 111–14; socioeconomic class and, 41

mysticism, 132

National Catholic Welfare Council, 111

National Christian Action Council, 58

National Congregations Study (NCS), 5, 15–16, 22, 84; diversity within congregations, 91–95, 92*fig*, 99

National Council of Churches, 111

nationalism, 17, 118, 121–24, 132

National Lutheran Council, 111

National Study of Youth and Religion (NSYR), 45

Neitz, Mary Jo, 37

Netherlands, trends in religion, 9

New Sanctuary Movement, 114

nones. *See* religiously unaffiliated (nones)

occupation, 128, 129; demographic shifts and, 70; demographic trends over time, 70–75, 72*fig*; gender and, 48. *See also* socioeconomic class

oppression, explanations for religious differences, 31–35

Palestine, 26

pastoral staff, diversity of, 91, 96

pastors. *See* clergy

Pentecostals: Black-White religious differences, 22; general trends in religion, 7–11, 8*fig*, 10*fig*

period effects, 63–67, 64*tab*; in American

religion, 57–58; cohort responses to, 62; defined, 56

Pew Research Center, 44, 61, 82, 112*fig*, 115

Pledge of Allegiance, 2

politics: 2016 presidential election, 102–3; African American Protestant churches and, 32–33; conservative Christianity and, 57–58; current debates, 132–33; drawing and defending boundaries, 106, 122–24; Protestant dominance, history of US and, 106–10; religion and racial hierarchies, 114–18; religious affiliation, overview of, 102–6, 104*fig*; sex and gender morality wars, 118–22, 119*fig*

poverty. *See* socioeconomic class

prayer: African American Protestant worship styles, 32–33; demographic trends over time, 78–79, 79*tab*; gender and, 44–48, 46*fig*; general trends in religion, 8; socioeconomic class and, 40–41, 40*fig*, 41*fig*; trends by race, gender, and education, 48–55, 50*fig*, 52*fig*, 53*fig*; trends by race over time, 28–29, 29*fig*

Presbyterians, 7, 39–40, 115

prohibition, 108–9

Proposition 187, California, 113

Protestant Reformation, 106–7

Protestants: 2016 presidential election and, 102–3; African America Protestantism, building blocks of, 32, 33; Asian American religious patterns, 24–25; Black-White religious differences, 21–23, 30–31; congregation size, trends in, 86–88; demographic trends over time, 70–75, 72*fig*; diversity within congregations, 94–95, 130–32; gender and religiousness, 47; general trends in religion, 6–11, 8*fig*, 10*fig*; Latinx trends over time, 29–31, 30*fig*; megachurches, 88–90; religion and racial hierarchies, 115–18; socioeconomic class and, 39–40, 40*fig*; use of term, 138n12. *See also* Black Protestantism; Evangelical Protestants; mainline Protestants

public education, 109, 117–18

Puritans, 106–7

Putnam, Robert, 57

race: Arab American religious patterns, 25–26; Asian American religious patterns, 23–25; Association of Religion Data Archives (ARDA), 35*box*; Black-White religious differences, 21–23;

race (*continued*)
demographic perspective on religion, 12–15, 126–30; demographic trends over time, 70–75, 72*fig*; diversity trends within congregations, 91–95, 92*fig*, 130–32; diversity within congregations, explanations and implications, 95–101; explanations for religious differences in, 31–35; Latinx religious patterns, 23; megachurches and, 89; migration rates, 68–70; prayer, trends over time, 78–79, 79*tab*; predicting future trends, 79–82; racial/ethnic groups, use of term, 20; racialization of religion, 35–36; religion and racial hierarchies, 114–18; Religious Right and, 121–22; religious trends, race, gender, and education, 48–55, 50*fig*, 52*fig*, 53*fig*; service attendance, trends over time, 76–77, 77*tab*; socioeconomic class and, 41–42; trends in religiousness over time, 26–29, 28*fig*, 29*fig*

Reagan, Ronald, 121

religion: definitions of, 2–5; demographic perspective on, 11–15; general trends in America, 6–11, 8*fig*, 10*fig*; racialization of, 35–36; survey data over time, 5–6. *See also* religiousness

Religion in Public, 120

religiously unaffiliated (nones), 137–38n11, 138n13; age, period, and cohort effects, 63–67, 64*tab*; demographic trends, overview, 129; future trends and challenges, 135; gender and, 44–47, 46*fig*; general trends in religion, 7–11, 8*fig*, 10*fig*; political identity and, 103–4, 104*fig*; as reaction to religious-based political activity, 58; socioeconomic class and, 40, 40*fig*; trends by race, gender, and education, 48–55, 50*fig*, 52*fig*, 53*fig*

religiousness: age effects, 58–60; Asian American population, 23–25; barriers to regular service participation, 43–44; Black-White religious differences, 21–23; cohort replacement, 63; definitions of, 3–5; education level and, 40–41, 40*fig*, 41*fig*; future trends and challenges, 133–35; gender and, 44–48, 46*fig*; Latinx population, 23; "lived religion," 127–28; period effects, 57–58; predicting future trends, 79–82; shifting demographic composition and, 67–70; trends by race, gender, and education, 48–55, 50*fig*, 52*fig*,

53*fig*; trends by race over time, 26–31, 28*fig*, 29*fig*, 30*fig*

Religious Right, 57, 118–22, 119*fig*

Religious Roundtable, 58

religious service attendance: Asian Americans population, 23–25; barriers to, 43–44; Black-White religious differences, 21–23; cohort replacement, 63; demographic trends over time, 75–78, 77*tab*, 126–30; gender and, 44–48, 46*fig*; general trends in religion, 8; Latinx population, 24; social conservatism and, 118–21, 119*fig*; socioeconomic class and, 40–41, 40*fig*, 41*fig*; trends by race, gender, and education, 48–55, 50*fig*, 52*fig*, 53*fig*; trends by race over time, 27–29, 28*fig*, 29*fig*

residential mobility, 69–70; demographic trends over time, 70–75, 72*fig*

residential stability, 69–70

risk aversion, religiousness and, 47

Roe v. Wade (1973), 121

Roosevelt, Theodore, 2

same-sex marriage, 118–22, 119*fig*

schools: desegregation and integration, 115–17; "In God We Trust," 2; Pledge of Allegiance, 2; public *vs.* private, 109, 117–18

secularization theory: demographic perspectives on, 12–15; overview of, 11–12

sexual morality wars, 118–22, 119*fig*

sexuality, 99, 119, 133

slavery, 114–15

spirituality, 3, 5, 57, 62, 132

Smith, Christian, 4

Smith, Joseph, 108

social capital, churches as source of, 34, 42–44

social conservatives, 118–22, 119*fig*

social media, politics and religion, 105

social mobility, religious groups and, 22, 34, 42–44, 69–70

social services/support: of African American churches, 22; African American Protestantism and, 32–33; in immigrant community churches, 34, 110; large *vs.* small congregations, 87–88; life cycle change in religiousness, 58–60

socioeconomic class: demographic perspective on religion, 13–14, 128, 130; explanations for religious differences, 31–35; Korean immigrants, 25; personal identity and, 38; religiousness and, 38–44, 40*fig*,

41*fig*; trends by race, gender, and education, 48–55, 50*fig*, 52*fig*, 53*fig*
Southern Baptists: on abortion rights, 121; general trends in religion, 7–11, 8*fig*, 10*fig*. *See also* Christianity;Evangelical Protestants
spirituality: alternative forms of, 57, 132; definitions of, 3–5; generational differences in, 62
surveys: general trends in religion in America, 6–11, 8*fig*, 10*fig*. *See also* General Social Survey (GSS); National Congregations Study (NCS); Pew Research Center
Syria, 26

tax-exempt status, 117
Trump, Donald, 102–3, 113, 121–22

unaffiliated. *See* religiously unaffiliated (nones)
United Service for New Americans, 111
United States, general trends in religion, 6–11, 8*fig*, 10*fig*
US Mint, 1–2

Vietnamese Americans, religious patterns, 23–25. *See also* Asian American population

Warren, Rick, 85

wealth: religious values and accumulation of wealth, 42–43. *See also* socioeconomic class
web-based religious communities, 131–32
Weber, Max, 42
White Christian nationalism, 17, 118, 121–24, 132
White Americans: Black-White religious differences, 21–23; demographic perspective on religion, 12–15, 126–30; diversity within congregations, 91–95, 92*fig*, 130–32; megachurches and, 89; religious trends, race, gender, and education, 48–55, 50*fig*, 52*fig*, 53*fig*; trends in religiousness over time, 27–29, 28*fig*, 29*fig*; use of term, 20
women: clergy trends, 91, 99; cultural expectations, 48–49; demographic perspective on religion, 13–14, 70–75, 72*fig*, 126–30; gender and religiousness, 44–48, 46*fig*; political morality wars, 118–22, 119*fig*; prayer, trends over time, 78–79, 79*tab*; religious trends, race, gender, and education, 37–38, 48–55, 50*fig*, 52*fig*, 53*fig*; service attendance, demographics of, 75–78, 77*tab*
World Values Survey, 8, 67

Yinger, J. Milton, 4

Founded in 1893,
UNIVERSITY OF CALIFORNIA PRESS
publishes bold, progressive books and journals
on topics in the arts, humanities, social sciences,
and natural sciences—with a focus on social
justice issues—that inspire thought and action
among readers worldwide.

The UC PRESS FOUNDATION
raises funds to uphold the press's vital role
as an independent, nonprofit publisher, and
receives philanthropic support from a wide
range of individuals and institutions—and from
committed readers like you. To learn more, visit
ucpress.edu/supportus.